Brooklyn Dodgers at Ebbets Field 1913-1957

Allen Schery

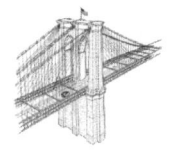

BROOKLYN BRIDGE BOOKS

Brooklyn Bridge Books

Bubbles

F ront Cover' (L to R)

Row One

Pee Wee Reese, Duke Snider, Gil Hodges, Roy Campanella

Row Two

Jackie Robinson, Carl Furillo, Carl Erskine, Don Newcombe

Row Three

Preacher Roe, Johnny Podres, Clem Labine

Above Ebbets Field

Charles Ebbets, Walter O'Malley, Branch Rickey

Back Cover (L to R)

Burleigh Grimes, Zack Wheat, Dazzy Vance, Leo Durocher

Copyright ©2025 by Allen Schery

All rights reserved.

ISBN : 978-1-968950-03-3

No portion of this book may be reproduced in any form without written permission from the publisher or author, except as permitted by U.S. copyright law.

Dedication

This book was not just words on a page; it was a journey through the most aching corners of my mind. Every sentence was a reliving of what felt like an unbelievable dream, the Golden Age of Dodger baseball, unfolding right outside my window and on WWOR channel 9 in New York.

That dream was shattered in 1957. I was just nine, a kid whose world revolved around my buddies, and then, in a blink, they were gone. They moved away, scattered like dust, and that raw, bewildered ache of abandonment I've carried with me ever since. How can anyone today truly grasp the soul of Brooklyn, the unbreakable sense of community that pulsed through its streets? Walter O'Malley wasn't just a man; he was the very embodiment of that spirit. He saw us, and he cared for us. My cherished 1955 autographed World Series team baseball, a gift from his own hand, is a testament to that profound connection passed on to me from my Aunt Marion. She was the Brooklyn Union Gas personnel director located at 195 Montague Street a few doors down from the Dodgers business office in the Mechanics Bank where Jackie Robinson actually signed his original contact---not Ebbets Field.

That legacy of care still lives on. His son, Peter O'Malley, a man of immense kindness, who stood beside me in the birthing of this book. Then there's Brent Shyer. I met him at Dodger Stadium in August of 1999 as the Dodgers brought me from Cooperstown to work on the Dodger Experience Museum at the stadium. Our connection was sports artist Scott Forst. Strangers at first he had warmth that instantly put me at ease, a smile, and a joke that brightened anyone's day. He became more than a contact; he was a steadfast ally, ensuring every single door was opened and every single wish granted, with a generosity that still hums. Also not to be forgotten Robert Schweppe, Peter's archivist, who spent hours delving into things I wasn't aware of and selflessly produced them, helping to make this book a team effort. All any of us wanted was unabated "truth" not unsupported soundbites that flooded the ether then and now.

I dedicate this book to these thoughtful, generous people who touched my life with their kindness and friendship. This book is for you. My gratitude, my deepest appreciation, echoes in every word right from my heart. We are still family, even after all those years as we both inexorably found our way to Los Angeles Peter.

Introduction
The Birth of a Brooklyn Cathedral

Baseball, that grand American symphony, has long been played upon fields that transcend mere dirt and grass. In Brooklyn, a borough brimming with life, hope, and a never-say-die attitude, the game found its most sacred ground in a ballpark forged not just of steel and cement, but of dreams. Ebbets Field—an endeavor born from the relentless ambition of Charles Ebbets, chiseled out of the roughest corners of Pigtown, and bound together by the unwavering faith of an entire city—stood not merely as a place where baseball was played, but where it was worshipped.

This was a house of miracles, a cathedral of the common man, where giants in cleats chased glory beneath the amber glow of Brooklyn sunsets. It was here, among the turnstiles and towering grandstands, that the Dodgers became more than a baseball team—they became the beating heart of a borough. Here, baseball wasn't just a pastime; it was a creed, a calling, a cause. From the moment the gates swung open, Brooklynites poured in, each one carrying their hopes like tickets clenched in eager hands. This was their home. Their hallowed ground.

The Dodgers were Brooklyn, and Brooklyn was the Dodgers. Their journey—one lined with triumphs and tragedies, heroes and heartbreakers—mirrored the borough itself, a land of resilience where struggle was expected and perseverance was celebrated. From the scrappy beginnings at Washington Park to the intoxicating roar of Ebbets Field, their story was one of ambition against impossible odds, of loyalty that never wavered, and of moments so electric they seemed to defy time itself.

In 1913, Brooklyn prepared itself for a transformation unlike any before—a rebirth in brick and limestone, a sanctuary where the old would give way to the new. The construction of Ebbets Field was more than a logistical undertaking; it was an act of faith. It was the embodiment of vision, of stubborn will, of Brooklyn's unshakable belief that the impossible could be made real.

No one could have foreseen the impact that this ballpark would have—not even Ebbets himself. Ashe stood upon the very ground where shanties and refuse once sprawled, he saw not the wasteland before him but the shining spectacle of what was to come. In his mind's eye, the hole in the ground transformed into a diamond. The ramshackle huts faded, replaced by towering stands packed with thousands upon thousands of voices that would one day cheer their team to glory.

What followed would be a tale worth telling—one of ambition, ingenuity, and the sheer stubbornness of men who refused to back down. Ebbets Field would become legendary, a place where memories were etched into every blade of grass, where unforgettable summers unfolded one pitch at a time, and where Brooklynites built their identity upon the successes and failures of their beloved Dodgers.

As the sun set over the borough in 1913, a new era was dawning. The gates of Ebbets Field were soon open, and within those walls, Brooklyn would find not just a ballpark, but a second home.

Contents

1. The Building of Ebbets Field — 1
2. Opening Daze — 8
3. Brooklyn Baseball Comes to Life (1916-1930) — 15
4. Through the Depression — 21
5. Three Early Dodger Hall of Famers — 27
6. World War II and the New Era (1941-1946) — 39
7. Jackie Robinson and Breaking Barriers (1947) — 47
8. Passing the Baton — 61
9. Larry MacPhail and the Transformation of the Brooklyn Dodgers (1938– 1942) — 68
10. The Tempestuous Leo Durocher — 75
11. Rickey and O'Malley — 81
12. The Road to Relocation (1946-1955) — 91
13. The Dodgers' Golden Age (1949-1956) — 102
14. It Comes Undone (1956-1957) — 136
15. Ebbets Field's End and Brooklyn's Loss (1958– 1960s) — 157

16. The Last Season at Ebbets Field – A Farewell to Brooklyn   164
    (1957)

17. Remembering Ebbets Field and the Brooklyn Dodgers   170

About the Author   178

Bibliography   180

Endnotes   188

Chapter One
The Building of Ebbets Field

At the end of 1908, as Brooklyn baseball stood on the precipice of change, Charles Ebbets faced the grim reality of his dwindling lease at Washington Park II. The ten-year agreement was expiring, and options were scarce. He had spent years fighting battles of rent, scrambling to secure a playable ground, and maneuvering through the financial gymnastics required to keep his beloved team afloat. He was not about to endure the same agony again—not on short notice, not with the stakes this high. Washington Park had been carved from necessity, but steel and cement were the future. Wood was outdated, a relic of baseball's past, a fire hazard looming over ballparks like a specter. No, this time, he would own the land outright and carve Brooklyn's baseball identity into something permanent.

However, permanence was expensive. Moving was still an idea more than a reality, and with the new season fast approaching, Ebbets had no choice but to extend the team's stay at Washington Park. A five-year lease, no option for renewal, would carry the club through the 1913 season. If Brooklyn were to move, it had to be by then.

By June 1909, Ebbets let slip a remark so nonchalant that few noticed its weight—Brooklyn would find land for a new park before 1913. The statement lacked urgency, but the process had already begun behind the scenes. The first parcel had been secured in September 1908, tucked away in the folds of Brooklyn's terrain, waiting for the pieces to fall into place.

Charles Hercules Ebbets

Rumors spread thick in 1911, whispers of the team returning to Eastern Park in East New York, speculation that carried no weight beyond its use as a smokescreen. The decision had already been made, though the location remained in flux.

While land was bought quietly, cash was hemorrhaging noisily. Gone was Gus Abell's financial safety net, and with it, Ebbets' ability to stave off disaster. He battled relentlessly against the rising tide of expenses, slashing salaries, begrudgingly approving pay raises, haggling with suppliers, and squeezing every dime passed through his hands. The ledger was a battlefield, and he micromanaged it with the desperation of a man staring down the possibility of ruin. Every ticket sold was dissected, and every financial transaction was examined with unwavering scrutiny. The only money he willingly let go of was the cash reserved for purchasing land.

It was all happening in fragments. The vision existed in Ebbets' mind, but the roadmap was jagged, incomplete, and uncertain. His first instinct was to remain at Washington Park, to purchase the land beneath it and reshape the ballpark's layout into something grander. Nevertheless, cost was an ever-present adversary, and after careful deliberation, he abandoned the plan and turned his attention elsewhere.

He scoured Brooklyn, combing its streets on foot, poring over maps, analyzing neighborhoods, considering transportation options, and weighing the logistical demands of a new stadium. Trolley lines, elevated trains, transfer points, and the arteries of movement through the borough were just as vital as the location.

Then came Pigtown

"Pigtown"

Two and a half miles from Washington Park, nestled in the bones of Flatbush, lay the unlikeliest candidates for baseball's next great cathedral. It was an eyesore, more ruin than promise, more refuse than potential. Squatters lived haphazardly across its expanse. A crater in the center scarred the land, a makeshift garbage dump that festered with the pungent remnants of discarded waste. His friends took one look and recoiled, questioning his sanity and judgment. They said the ballpark would be too far from South Brooklyn, Park Slope, Williamsburg, and Greenpoint. The skepticism was absolute.

Ebbets ignored them.

Thirty-odd parcels comprised the space that would become Ebbets Field and securing them required maneuvering between proper deeds and squatters' rights, between landowners and uncertainty. His attorney Bernard J. York and his real estate agent Howard Pyle advised secrecy, warning that any announcement would skyrocket prices. A shell corporation—the Pylon Construction Company—was formed to obscure his intentions. However, amused by the irony, fate allowed the cover to slip when sellers noticed that the purchasing entity resembled Pyle's real estate company. Assumptions were made, numbers inflated, and prices surged.

The land was acquired for $200,000—half in cash, half in notes. A two-year, $100,000 loan from the Mechanics Bank in New York bolstered the transaction. The foundation was set, but the ballpark remained a dream without the means to build it.

And then, the last missing piece—the final land parcel.

The problem? No one could find the owner.

Stories diverged, tangled in contradiction. He had gone to Berlin—or maybe the Alps. Some claimed he had ventured to Paris. Others doubted he had ever left New York. Eventually, whispers led investigators to California—unless he had never been there at all. Montclair, New Jersey, was dragged into the saga, though how or why was never fully explained. Finally, after a labyrinthine pursuit worthy of myth, the man surfaced, delighted that someone was interested in his land.

At first, $500 seemed fair. Nevertheless, with the swirling buzz surrounding the project, it was worth more. The asking price doubled to $2,000, and with no alternative, Ebbets paid it. The last piece of the puzzle locked into place.

Ebbets Field nearing completion in 1913. Note that no one lived there at the time, and house from "Pigtown" is seen on the left.

Construction officially began in March 1912, but Brooklyn's brutal winter had frozen the ground nearly three feet deep, causing delays. The press was merciless, describing the site as "pleasantly diversified" with "picturesque homes of squatters" and likening the hole in the middle to "the subway to China." Critics doubted whether the land could ever be transformed into a ballpark, but Ebbets remained undeterred.

Ebbets fought for control. He negotiated, micromanaged, and cut costs wherever possible. But reality set in. He was losing his grip, losing himself to exhaustion, and his doctor noticed.

The prescription was simple—leave, or break.

Thus, begrudgingly, he boarded a ship for New Orleans, stepping away from the ballpark he had fought to build. He had little choice. His body was failing him, and Brooklyn would have to continue without him.

Model T Ford flies by on Bedford Avenue near Ebbets Field in 1913.

The grand opening was magnificent chaos. Crowds surged, ushers scrambled, reporters dissected every imperfection with ruthless precision. Yet, standing in the rotunda, Ebbets absorbed it all—every moment, every doubt, every battle that had led him to this day. He had gambled everything on this ballpark; now, it was his.

The skeptics had laughed when he claimed baseball was still in its infancy. Nevertheless, Charles Ebbets had seen what they had not. He had told his daughter, Lydie Mae, that if she lived long enough, she would witness Ebbets Field becoming too small and that the Dodgers would leave Brooklyn one day entirely.

Forty-four years later, history would prove him right.

For now, though, he stood in the ballpark that bore his name, weary but victorious, knowing that against all odds, he had won.

Chapter Two
Opening Daze

In the tender glow of an early April dawn, Brooklyn awoke to a day foretold by destiny and daring—a day when the hallowed gates of the magnificent, state-of-the-art Ebbets Field would swing open to an ocean of hopes and histories. The frigid consternation was etched upon the resolute faces of Charles Ebbets and the ever-watchful McKeevers, their expressions a storm of mingled anxiety and jubilant anticipation. For these pioneers, whose dreams had been tempered in the crucible of the National League's labyrinthine ownership web, the morning was imbued with both trepidation and transcendent promise.

A tempest of intricate negotiations and power plays had been weathered, as every magnate preened and postured in pursuit of his glittering fortunes. In this charged milieu, a momentous triumph emerged: the beleaguered Brooklyn team, against all odds, secured the honor of staging an exhibition game with the formidable New York Yankees. It is worth noting that the Yankees of that era had not yet been reshaped by the legendary influence of beer money and ambition; indeed, in 1913, they shared the Polo Grounds with the Giants and would not unveil the splendor of Yankee Stadium until 1922. Every detail of this saga, every ripple and resonance of its unfolding, stands as a testament to an age when the beauty of baseball was interwoven with the grand ideals of progress and passion.

In those days, sports journalism was a dazzling art form, a riotous collage of imaginative, colorful, capricious, ingenious, and flamboyant verbiage that danced boldly across the pages of local newspapers. These print epics, composed with an impulsive, whimsical verve, transformed mundane reports into lyrical narratives. With an insatiable hunger for diverse perspectives, families devoured four or more newspapers each week, reveling in the array of alternative versions of every momentous event. With no radio or television to capture the instant essence of the spectacle, each report was a crafted masterpiece, and its every line was a vibrant portrait meant to ignite the reader's imagination and spirit.

As the morning matured, the heavens conspired to cast a benevolent light over the day. Contrary to whispered warnings of overnight rain, the skies unveiled one of the most crystalline and delightful spring days that the venerable residents of Brooklyn—and especially those of the mellifluous "Pigtown"—could ever recall. There was an ineffable charm in the gentle warmth of the sun and the expansive blue vault overhead; together, they spoke of rebirth, delightful serendipity, and the promise of sporting glory.

Nevertheless, amid the rhapsodic incandescence of nature, an even greater test lay in wait—the orchestration of a transportation marvel that would usher an unruly cavalcade of over 10,000 ardent souls to the newly minted coliseum. Driven by the thrill of the occasion, Charles Ebbets seemed to have enlisted the assistance of the spirited Mack Senett and his whimsical band of "Keystone Cops." A journey to the park then was an odyssey—a muddy escapade where rutted roads and overburdened trolleys and trains groaned under the collective weight of exuberance. The Brighton and Fulton elevated lines, laden as if by some invisible hand with the compressed energy of jubilant patriots, seemed to whisper in mechanical agony. Each carriage, every overcrowded compartment, pulsed with eager excitement and the promise of communal celebration. Even the sporadic—and then scarce—automobiles added modern splendor to the grand motor display, captivating onlookers who mused, with a hint of wry Brooklynese humor, that "there ain't that many machines made."

Through every conceivable mode of conveyance, the hurrying, chatty, and effervescent horde converged upon the majestic gates of Ebbets Field. The grand rotunda, with its lofty 80-foot arch, echoed the dreams and ambitions of the city. It stood as a veritable portal to a realm where the mundane transformed into the extraordinary. Within these hallowed chambers, throngs of beaming fans were ushered past ticket counters that swung open like the mighty sluice gates of a dam, releasing wave after wave of ardent admirers into the arena. The ingenious introduction of ramps—an innovation notably absent at Washington Park II—heralded a new era of architectural and logistical brilliance.

Amid this animated spectacle, scribes poised their quills to capture the splendor and chaos with a fervor that rivaled the drama unfolding before their eyes. Their ink flowed in rich cascades as they recorded the "hearty shouts of approval" and the collective wonder elicited by that first sweeping glimpse of Ebbets' grand new enterprise. For Brooklyn, that day was far more than a baseball game; it was an ode to communal triumph, an artistic celebration of beauty emerging from both order and delightful disorder.

However, for all its magnificent perfection, the day was not without its whimsically endearing imperfections. A single, charming misadventure, the misplacement of a vital flag, was destined to become an anecdote for the ages. At the preordained hour of 3:00 PM, when the esteemed owners gathered to imbue the ceremony with stately grace, Charles Ebbets strode with dignified determination toward the flagpole, flanked by Ed and Jenny McKeever. In a moment of comically human oversight reminiscent of a Groucho Marx escapade from "Horsefeathers," no flag awaited them; it had been inadvertently abandoned in the clutter of Ebbets' office. As Shannon's Band rendered the stirring strains of the "Star Spangled Banner," a half-hour delay ensued, during which young Genevieve Ebbets—Charlie's cherished daughter—took up the mantle to throw out the first ball, wisely avoiding any confusion with her father's oversized bowling balls.

Ed McKeever, Charles H. Ebbets watch Genevieve Ebbets throw out first ball.

Then, as if choreographed by fate's whimsical script, the game emerged—a brief and profoundly electric contest at once. Initially, Brooklyn surged ahead with a dazzling two-run lead, courtesy of acrobatic inside-the-park home runs by the promising rookie Casey Stengel and stalwart first baseman Jake Daubert. Nevertheless, in a twist imbued with the capricious humor of fate—a scene reminiscent of a W. C. Fields film—the Brooklyn pitcher, Frank Allen, relinquished control of the ball in the top of the ninth inning, allowing the Yankees to tie the score with audacious flair. This unforeseen turn set the stage for a finale that might well have leapt off the pages of a "Flash Gordon" saga: Future hall-of-famer Zach Wheat, propelled by the indefatigable drive of Carlisle Smith, powered home for a walk-off victory that transformed an ordinary contest into an eternal epic. As the game reached its dazzling crescendo, the fans' elation swelled to such a degree that special contingents of police and firefighters were summoned to tame the ensuing exodus—a veritable ballet of order and chaos amid the twilight of celebration

Hall of Famer Casey Stengel

No new ballpark escapes the vicissitudes of its inaugural days, and Ebbets Field was no exception. The imposed limitations of its 24,000 seats—falling a full 10,000 short of the zealous throng—sparked a spirited scramble among devoted fans. Ingenious and intrepid, they sought every possible vantage point: from the lofty overlook across Montgomery Street near the forlorn Crow Hill Penitentiary to hastily assembled, rickety stands fashioned by local amateur architects with the bold ambition to hold "300 or more." Some risked "breaking their necks" in pursuit of a distant glimpse of the unfolding drama, whether from houses, beneath barns, among ancient trees, or atop recalcitrant telegraph poles. In these moments, the term "fan" transcended its ordinary meaning and celebrated instead an impassioned fanatic- a soul determined to imprint his love for the game upon the annals of history.

Even as this grand pageant of public revelry unfolded, the true spectacle-the game itself—remained a subtle backdrop and a fervent focal point.

The afternoon's proceedings were not merely a contest of athletic prowess, but a rich tapestry interwoven with innovation, serendipity, and the palpable spirit of communal unity. Every pitch, every thunderous cheer, and every miscalculated throw was captured by loyal chroniclers, determined to immortalize the day's ineffable magic

In the end, as the resplendent day waned and twilight's luminous hues embraced Brooklyn, the legacy of Ebbets Field's opening was indelibly sealed. The game, with its dramatic walk-off finish and moments of unforeseen hilarity, served as the triumphant culmination of an experience that transcended the realm of sport. It was a day when the dreams of a city were realized in vivid color—a day when every puddle of mud, every groaning trolley, and every meticulously crafted newspaper column bore witness to the unyielding passion undergirding America's pastime.

Hall of Famer Zack Wheat

Thus, in all its sprawling, adjective-laced magnificence, "Opening Daze" was not merely a demonstration of athletic competition. It was an epic, a lyrical celebration of ambition and community, a day when Brooklyn's air shimmered with promise—a testament to the ingenuity of humankind, the enduring power of collective celebration, and the timeless allure of baseball.

One might think that the story ended here, but the lightning ending left fans trying to figure out how to get out of Ebbets Field, which generated "no little commotion." Special police and firemen had to come to the fans' aid.

No new ballpark was devoid of glitches. The biggest problems were the lack of entrances and ticket lines, which kept people who had already bought tickets from entering the park. The 80-foot rotunda was too small. Shortly thereafter, Ebbets remedied the situation by adding four new ticket entrances and allowing an exit point in centerfield. There would be more drama in the 44 years of life the park had left. It would have a dramatic, unexpected ending. Nonetheless, at least for that day, everybody went home happy.

Chapter Three
Brooklyn Baseball Comes to Life (1916-1930)

The summer of 1916 was a gilded season, where hope soared and fate wavered, a fleeting moment of glory that shimmered like the setting sun over Ebbets Field. Ever the mastermind, Charles Ebbets knew his Dodgers had assembled a team capable of hoisting a National League pennant—but only once. Their fragile and brilliant championship window aligned perfectly with the storm clouds looming on the horizon—World War I and financial uncertainty.

Brooklyn, that borough of grit and devotion, felt its pulse quicken as the Dodgers stormed through the National League, claiming their first-ever trip to the World Series, which had started in 1903. The world beckoned them to the grand stage—a battle against the mighty Boston Red Sox, where legends roamed and history waited. But despite their fire, Brooklyn found itself staring down the indomitable figure of Babe Ruth, a colossus upon the mound. The fight was valiant, the struggle fierce, but destiny proved unkind. Ruth and his companions sent Brooklyn home empty-handed in five games, the weight of near-glory settling like dust upon their uniforms.

From Author's Dodger Museum Collection

Brooklyn's faithful, ever loyal yet accustomed to heartbreak, did not waver. They carried the burden of loss with a smirk and a shrug, their devotion a badge of honor. The underdog Dodgers, scrappy and resilient, embodied the borough itself—a place where dreams fought for survival and laughter held hands with misfortune. In these years of toil and triumph, the famed "Dem Bums" culture took root, forged in struggle, bound by loyalty.

Brooklyn baseball was more than a spectacle—a hymn sung in the streets, a rhythm woven into the city's fabric. The Dodgers' victories sent vendors scrambling, shopkeepers bracing for crowds, saloons packed with patrons dissecting every pitch over whiskey and roast beef. Newspapers chronicled each twist and turn with prose as fevered as the fans themselves, while radio—entering the picture in the roaring twenties—brought the game's drama to the ears of those too far to see the dust rise from home plate.

Brooklyn baseball was an adhesive, binding together the working-class borough with an unspoken understanding. Losses stung, but victories were shared, carried aloft like trophies in the hearts of every man, woman, and child who dared to dream alongside their Dodgers. The murmurs of "Dem Bums" became a rallying cry, a promise between the team and its people: no matter how often fate intervened, Brooklyn would endure.

As seasons changed, so too did fortunes. Player salaries skyrocketed after the Federal League war, Ebbets stretched his budget to its limits, and his frugal ways earned him scorn among players who wanted their due. Casey Stengel, a wily strategist with firein his soul, battled Ebbets for recognition, his words sharp as a curveball break. Zach Wheat, ever the silent force, chose dignity over dispute—but evensilence had its consequences. Frustrated Ebbets took his grievances to the press, stirring tensions that simmered just below the surface.

The war in Europe soon Cast its long shadow over baseball's golden fields. Wartime taxes drained profits, players departed for service, and stadiums became staging grounds for supplies. Once a haven of cheers and curses, Brooklyn was entwined with history's relentless march.

By 1918, the government issued the infamous "Work or Fight" order as war reached itscrescendo. Baseball had no choice but to yield. The Red Sox were crowned champions in an abbreviated season, and Ebbets Field fell silent, transformed into a depot for war materials.

Ebbets, ever the gambler, refused to accept defeat. He staged a patriotic concert, a thinly veiled attempt to circumvent Sunday baseball laws. But the law stood firm—his charade was revealed, and with it came arrest, controversy, and a storm of headlines. Yet amid the chaos, progress crept forward. The battle for Sunday baseball had begun to tip toward victory.

While the players evolved, so too did their battleground. Ebbets Field, once a modest structure, grew with the passing years. Wooden bleachers yielded to concrete, sightlines sharpened, and amenities expanded. But even in its renewal, the ballpark remained intimate, beloved for its closeness, for the voices of its fans rising like atide against the cavernous halls of its rivals.

The borough's devotion returned with force as Brooklyn emerged from the war. The repeal of blue laws in 1919 brought fresh waves of fans through the turnstiles, and with them came a swell of optimism. The Dodgers flourished, their resilience propelling them to the grand stage again in 1920. Yet controversy, that ever-present specter, loomed over baseball once again.

Brooklyn, preparing for battle against Cleveland, found itself entangled in scandal. Rube Marquard, veteran pitcher with years of wisdom in his arm, stepped into the Winton Hotel, thinking little of what lay ahead. He offered a friend overpriced tickets, unaware that his words carried weight beyond intention. A detective overheard, an arrest followed, and soon, 400 reporters spun a tale of scandal that echoed across the sport.

The timing was cruel. The wounds of the 1919 Black Sox scandal still bled, and baseball, fragile in its integrity, could not afford another scar. Charles Ebbets and the McKeevers, furious at the stain on Brooklyn's name, acted swiftly. Marquard was sent to Cincinnati that winter, his Hall of Fame years still ahead, but his time in Brooklyn abruptly ended.

Rube Marquard (Courtesy Charles Mandel-Helmar Brewing Company)

The series unfolded like an epic, a clash of titans with fortunes teetering on the edge. Brooklyn struck first, then Cleveland roared back. And then, in Game 5, history held its breath—a triple play—the rarest of feats, executed like poetry in motion. Bill Wambsganss, moving like a maestro before a stunned audience, turned three outs in a single stroke. The Dodgers reeled. The dream slipped away.

Battered by financial struggles and controversy, Ebbets pressed forward into the decade. His club, riddled with defensive shortcomings, lacked a true shortstop—a problem that would not be solved until the arrival of Pee Wee Reese years later.

By 1924, years of strain had worn Ebbets down. His breath labored, his steps slowed, yet he refused to relinquish his hold. The battles, now fought over contracts with Burleigh Grimes and Dazzy Vance, drained what little strength remained.

On April 18, 1925, Charles Ebbets passed away, his body yielding to time and toil. His funeral drew friends, family, and the Brooklyn faithful, mourning the man who had given them their beloved team. But tragedy was not yet done. Ed McKeever, grieving his longtime friend, fell ill at Ebbets' funeral. Within a week, he too was gone.

Charles Ebbets, Wilbert Robinson, Steve & Ed McKeever

Chapter Four
Through the Depression

Brooklyn, that sacred borough where baseball was not merely played but lived, endured years between 1925 and 1940 where victory seemed a foreign concept, obscured behind layers of strife, mismanagement, and unrelenting familial discord. The Dodgers, that once-proud institution clad in the unmistakable blue and white, stumbled through these years like a heavyweight fighter past his prime, absorbing one blow after another without ever countering, dragging through the standings as though chained to the inertia of their dysfunction.

Ebbets Field, the once-glorious coliseum where Brooklyn hearts beat strongest, suffered alongside its inhabitants—the rotunda, once a gleaming entryway welcoming thousands, grew mottled with mildew and neglect. The wooden seats groaned beneath the weight of time, some splintered, some sagging, all reflecting the decay that had come to define the organization itself. The bathrooms, long forgotten by maintenance crews, fell into disrepair, the pipes gurgling up what little remained of their usefulness before succumbing entirely. And by 1937, the silence of disconnected telephone lines echoed through the halls—unpaid bills sealing off communication, leaving the Dodgers' front office as barren as the franchise's hopes.

But behind the walls of Ebbets Field, the actual theater of tragedy unfolded. For fifteen years, Brooklyn's greatest adversaries were not the Giants, the Cardinals, or any team that stood in opposition on the playing field—their most formidable foes resided within their ownership, men so entangled in personal vendettas that winning became secondary, a casualty of ceaseless strife.

Unyielding in principle and inflexible in judgment, Steve McKeever loomed over the franchise like an unforgiving warden, wielding his authority with more fervor for personal battles than baseball itself. He was a man who saw moral failings not as missteps but as outright sins, who viewed ownership less as a stewardship over a team than as a pulpit from which to enact his righteous campaign. And at the center of his scorn stood Charles Ebbets Jr., heir to a legacy that Steve deemed undeserving. Their hatred was not simply a disagreement—it was war.

Charles Ebbets Jr.

McKeever believed Ebbets Jr. embodied everything that corrupted tradition. The bitterness reached an extraordinary boiling point when Charles Jr., still holding rank as club secretary and part-owner, was physically ejected from his stadium—not once, but twice. Seeing an heir to the Dodgers being forcibly removed from the ballpark that bore his father's name was an astonishing display of contempt that spilled from boardroom disputes into a public spectacle. The lawsuits followed, not in search of resolution, but of retribution, and ownership became entangled in leadership and vengeance. While baseball teams battled for pennants, Brooklyn battled itself, firing legal challenges instead of fastballs, wielding grudges instead of drafting players.

Thus, the Dodgers remained locked in place, dragging through a mire of sixth-place finishes year after year; their fate was predetermined by forces beyond their control. On the rare occasion they ascended to third place, it was not because of a clear vision or strategic prowess—it was mere happenstance, a fluke within the churn of dysfunction. Players came, players went, and managers were reshuffled like pieces on a chessboard where no one could see the entire game. Baseball, once the beating heart of Brooklyn, became a side note to a far uglier tale.

The Great Depression sank its talons into the sport, forcing teams to innovate or perish. Stadium attendance shriveled, profits faded, and survival became the only goal. Radio broadcasts carried the game's sounds into the living rooms of fans who could no longer afford a seat at the ballpark. Night games illuminated stadiums desperate for revenue, hoping to entice workers off long shifts into late-evening entertainment. Farm systems expanded, offering a cheaper means to develop talent and maintain rosters. But in Brooklyn, no adaptation could fix what had been broken from within. The Dodgers were not merely struggling due to the Depression's financial strains—they were already failing under the weight of their chaos.

"Uncle" Wilbert Robinson, Manager if Brooklyn "Robins" 1913-1931. In 1932 Dodger name was put on the uniforms.

Wilbert "Uncle Robbie" Robinson remained constant throughout the storm, his managerial reign stretching over decades. He carried warmth within the clubhouse, a familiarity that stood in contrast to the bitter battles in ownership. But with each passing year, his control slipped through his fingers, lost in the currents of leadership that had long ceased to prioritize baseball itself. McKeever, convinced that Robinson was a liability, seized upon an opportunity to oust him, branding him "the Squealer" with venom in his voice, his disdain culminating in rage so tangible it led to the infamous ink-well incident—an act of fury that forced Robinson to abandon his own office and retreat to a small corner of the ballpark, a man in exile within his domain.

When the final blow came in 1931, Robinson did not resist. He did not plead. He did not bargain for reconsideration. The news reached him as he fished along the waters near Butler Island, Georgia. When he heard it, he merely let go—first of his net, sinking into the depths as irretrievable as his career, and later of his dignity, drowning it in whiskey. His sorrow did not manifest as words—it flowed with each poured drink. He was not a man ruined in the traditional sense, but a man who had seen his purpose erased. Three years later, he was dead.

Brooklyn did not mourn, and the Dodgers, as an institution, did not pause in reflection. The machine churned forward, leaving Robinson behind like it had abandoned its stability.

Meanwhile, Ebbets Field fell further into disrepair, each broken plank and rusting fixture a reminder of how far the franchise had fallen. Bills stacked higher, debts stretched wider, and process servers haunted the gates like specters, demanding payments for an organization that had long forgotten fiscal responsibility. The faithful fans still arrived, their love unwavering, but their devotion was repaid only with disappointment.

Then came the fire. Then came Leo Durocher.

Durocher entered the Brooklyn landscape like an approaching storm, electrifying a team that had known only stagnation. His philosophy was brash, relentless, borderline ruthless. "Nice guys finish last," he declared, and Brooklyn, weary of finishing last, took notice. His arrival did not immediately mend the wounds of the past, nor did it bring victories overnight, but it injected into the Dodgers something they had lacked for far too long: identity.

And then, at last, the past breathed its last breath.

Steve McKeever, the self-proclaimed moral warden of Brooklyn baseball, passed away in March 1938. His departure carried more weight than any roster change and more significance than any managerial shift. With him went the final barrier to reform, and in the wake of his absence, the Brooklyn Trust Company took hold. No more debts left unchecked, no more chaos ruling unchecked.

Larry MacPhail arrived not with promises, but with action. Where Brooklyn had faltered, he accelerated. Where leadership had crumbled, he built. For the first time in over a decade, Brooklyn's horizon was not clouded in mismanagement and spite—it was clear.

And while the wounds of fifteen years did not fade overnight, the Dodgers were reborn.

Brooklyn, wounded and weary, still stood. The fans who had endured every loss and suffered through every indignity still filled the stands. They had never abandoned their team. And now, at long last, their faith would be rewarded.

Because Brooklyn, at its core, was never meant to remain beaten.

Brooklyn was meant to rise.

Chapter Five
Three Early Dodger Hall of Famers

Zack Wheat

Zachariah Davis "Zack" Wheat (1888-1972), often affectionately known by his nickname "Buck," was a truly prominent figure in early 20th-century baseball. He carved out a remarkable 19-season career primarily as a graceful and consistent left fielder for the Brooklyn Dodgers. Wheat was renowned for his smooth left-handed swing and exceptional defensive abilities, leaving an indelible mark on the sport that culminated in his well-deserved induction into the National Baseball Hall of Fame.

Born on May 23, 1888, in Hamilton, Missouri, Zack Wheat embarked on his professional baseball journey in the minor leagues, playing for various teams, including Fort Worth, Shreveport, and Mobile. While his early minor league batting averages might not have been spectacular, he quickly established a strong reputation for his defensive skills in the outfield. This talent caught the eye of Brooklyn scout Larry Sutton, leading to Wheat's acquisition by the Brooklyn Superbas (who would later evolve into the Dodgers and Robins) in August 1909 for $1,200. He made his highly anticipated Major League debut on September 11, 1909, and immediately made an impression, batting an impressive .304 in just 26 games during that initial season.

Wheat dedicated most of his 18-season career to the Brooklyn franchise, where he became a beloved and enduring fixture. He was a cornerstone of the team through its various iterations—Superbas, Dodgers, and Robins—and was widely recognized for his quiet demeanor and consistently high performance. Indeed, legendary manager Casey Stengel once remarked of Wheat, "One of the grandest guys ever to wear a baseball uniform, one of the greatest batting teachers I have ever seen, one of the truest pals a man ever had, and one of the kindliest men God ever created." The initial phase of Wheat's career unfolded during baseball's "Dead Ball Era," characterized by notably lower offensive numbers due to less lively baseballs. Despite these challenging conditions, Wheat consistently ranked among the league's elite hitters. From 1912 to 1916, he was a regular presence among the league leaders in home runs, which was a significant accomplishment given how rare double-digit home run totals were then. His standout season during this particular period occurred in 1914 when he achieved a .319 batting average, complemented by 26 doubles, nine triples, and nine home runs. His strong performance that year earned him a ninth-place finish in MVP voting. A significant highlight of his Dead Ball Era contributions was the 1916 season. Wheat batted an impressive .312 and notably led the National League in total bases and slugging percentage. He also set a Brooklyn franchise record by extending his hitting streak to 29 games, a performance that undoubtedly helped the Robins clinch the National League pennant that year. They faced the formidable Boston Red Sox in the ensuing World Series, ultimately losing four games to one. Wheat achieved his sole batting title in 1918, hitting an impressive

.335. This mark was his highest average up to that point in his career, and it was particularly remarkable considering he hit no home runs that season, further underscoring his exceptional pure-hitting ability during a pitching-dominated era.

T-206 1909-1911 Zack Wheat from Authors Dodger Museum Collection

With the advent of the "lively ball" in the 1920s, many players experienced a significant surge in their offensive output, and Zack Wheat proved to be no exception. Despite being in his early 30s when this fundamental change occurred, he seamlessly adapted his game and thrived. Starting in 1919, Wheat was appointed captain of the Robins, a testament to his leadership. From 1920 to 1925, he consistently maintained an exceptional .347 batting average. During this period, he notably recorded three 200-hit seasons in his mid-30s, a testament to his sustained hitting prowess. He reached double-digit home runs for the first time in 1921 with 14, a feat he would repeat thrice over the next four years. His offensive peak during the lively ball era included hitting an astounding .375 in consecutive seasons (1923 and 1924). While he did not lead the league in batting average in either of these years, Rogers Hornsby posted even higher averages, and Wheat's remarkable consistency and sustained high performance were undeniable. In 1924, at 36, he finished a respectable third in the NL MVP voting, also placed second in the league in batting average, OPS, doubles, total bases, and hits. The Robins made another World Series appearance in 1920 but ultimately fell to the Cleveland Indians five games to two. Despite the team's overall loss, Wheat maintained his strong hitting, batting .333 in the series.

Beyond his consistent prowess at the plate, Wheat was equally renowned for his exceptional fielding in left field. He possessed a strong arm and exhibited a graceful, highly efficient style of play. He notably led National League left fielders in putouts an impressive seven times throughout his career (1913, 1914, 1915, 1916, 1919, 1924, and 1925). Furthermore, he twice led the league in fielding percentage (1918 and 1922). Baseball Magazine famously lauded him in 1917, stating, "What Lajoie was to infielders, Zack Wheat is to outfielders, the finest mechanical craftsman of them all. Wheat is the easiest, most graceful of outfielders with no close rivals." This praise highlighted his remarkable defensive consistency and skill. Despite his overall robustness, Wheat, who wore a small 5 1/2 shoe, was occasionally prone to nagging ankle injuries.

Across 2,410 games over his 19-season career, Zack Wheat compiled awe-inspiring and comprehensive statistics: a batting average of .317, 2,884 hits, 1,289 runs, 476 doubles, 172 triples, 132 home runs, 1,248 runs batted in (RBI), 205 stolen bases, an on-base percentage (OBP) of .367, and a slugging percentage (SLG) of .450. These figures underscore his consistent offensive production and overall impact. Wheat holds the Brooklyn/Los Angeles Dodgers' all-time franchise leadership in several key offensive categories, including games played, at-bats, plate appearances, hits, doubles, triples, and total bases, solidifying his legacy as a team icon. His career was also marked by unique moments, such as his participation in a marathon 26-inning, 1-1 tie game against the Boston Braves in 1920 and a peculiar home run where the ball reportedly lodged in a flag in right field before falling onto the field, a ruling upheld by the National League President.

The Dodgers released Wheat on New Year's Day, 1927, marking the end of his long tenure with the team. He subsequently signed with the Philadelphia Athletics for his final Major League season. There, he batted a respectable .324 in 62 games. He served as a pinch-hitter and outfielder on an Athletics team that boasted multiple .300 hitters, including baseball legends like Ty Cobb and Al Simmons. Following this, he briefly played in the American Association in 1928 before retiring from professional baseball. After his illustrious playing career concluded, Wheat returned to his farm in Missouri. It is an interesting historical note that he had famously raised and sold mules to the U.S. Army during World War I, a shrewd off-season business venture he would often leverage during contract negotiations. The onset of the Great Depression, however, forced him to sell his farm in 1932. Subsequently, he relocated to Kansas City, Missouri, where he operated a bowling alley. In a later chapter of his life, he transitioned into a career as a police officer.

Zack Wheat was deservedly inducted into the National Baseball Hall of Fame in 1959 by the Veterans Committee. His election profoundly recognized his consistent excellence as a hitter, exceptional defensive skills, and remarkable longevity in the game. He was remembered as a quiet, unassuming star performing at an elite level for nearly two decades, leaving a profound legacy as one of his era's finest outfielders and purest hitters.

His enduring franchise records for the Dodgers underscore his indelible importance to the team's rich history and Major League Baseball.

Burleigh Grimes

Burleigh Arland Grimes (1893-1985), famously known as "Ol' Stubblebeard" for his intimidating, unshaven presence on the mound, was a legendary figure in Major League Baseball. He was celebrated not only for his remarkable longevity and fierce competitiveness but also for being the last pitcher legally permitted to throw the spitball. His illustrious 19-year career left an indelible mark on the sport, culminating in his well-deserved induction into the National Baseball Hall of Fame.

Born on August 18, 1893, in Emerald, Wisconsin, Grimes grew up in a lumbering family, developing an early passion for baseball. After his father's passing, he worked in a lumber camp to support his family, an experience that likely contributed to his burly physique and tenacious spirit. Standing 5'10" and weighing 175 lbs, he was a "burly" fellow. He began his professional career in the minor leagues in 1912, learning and perfecting the art of spitball. Unlike many pitchers, Grimes held the ball tightly and moistened it with slippery elm bark, enabling his pitches to break with unusual and deceptive movement, often deceiving hitters by seven or eight inches. After several successful minor league seasons, he made his Major League debut with the Pittsburgh Pirates in September 1916. His initial stint with the Pirates was challenging; in 1917, he endured a tough season that included an unfortunate 13 straight losses, contributing to his 3-16 record. However, a trade to the Brooklyn Robins (later Dodgers) before the 1918 season dramatically turned his career around.

"Ole' stubble-beard" Burleigh Grimes-Last legal spitball pitcher 1909-1911 t-206 from authors Dodger Museum Collection

In Brooklyn, Grimes quickly established himself as a premier pitcher. In his first season with the Robins in 1918, he posted an impressive 19-9 record despite serving in the Navy for most of that season. He and teammate Rube Marquard were assigned to a recruiting station in Chicago but were notably permitted to pitch for Brooklyn. A pivotal moment in his career and baseball history came in February 1920 when Major League Baseball outlawed the spitball. However, Grimes and 16 other established pitchers were granted an exemption, allowing him to continue throwing the pitch until his retirement. This unique status cemented his place in baseball lore. With his signature pitch still legal, Grimes helped lead the Brooklyn Robins to the National League pennant in 1920, where he recorded a stellar 23-11 record and a 2.22 ERA. He proved to be a dominant force throughout the early 1920s, logging multiple 20-win seasons for Brooklyn, including 22 wins in 1921, when he also led the league in wins and strikeouts. He also led the National League in complete games three times (1921, 1923, 1924) and innings pitched twice (1923, 1924).

After a successful tenure with the Dodgers, Grimes's career saw him move through several teams in the latter half of his playing days, including the New York Giants, Pittsburgh Pirates (again), Boston Braves, St. Louis Cardinals, Chicago Cubs, and New York Yankees. His second stint with the Pirates in 1928 was particularly notable, as he led the National League with 25 wins, 48 games, 28 complete games, and 330.2 innings pitched.

ALLEN SCHERY

In 1931, as a member of the St. Louis Cardinals, Grimes achieved his only World Series championship. Demonstrating his legendary toughness, he famously pitched 8 1/3 innings. He won in Game 7 to clinch the series victory against the Philadelphia Athletics despite reportedly suffering a dislocated vertebra before the game. He appeared in four World Series (1920, 1930, 1931, 1932). His unyielding competitive spirit was a hallmark of his time on the mound; "Only one man was standing between me and more money," Grimes famously said, "and that was the guy with the bat." He was known for glaring at infielders who made errors and sneering at umpires, earning him a reputation as a "snarling, hard-to-get-along-with personality" while pitching. He was known to be talkative and thoughtful off the field; however, he often shared his insights on pitching techniques.

By his retirement in 1934, Grimes had amassed an impressive career record of 270 wins against 212 losses, with a 3.53 ERA and 1,512 strikeouts over 4,180 innings pitched. He completed 314 of his 497 starts and recorded 35 shutouts. A surprisingly good hitter for a pitcher, he posted a career .248 batting average with 168 RBIs. His retirement marked the end of an era, as he was the last of the 17 exempted pitchers to throw the spitball legally.

After his playing career, Grimes remained deeply involved in baseball. He managed the Brooklyn Dodgers in 1937 and 1938, even having Babe Ruth as one of his coaches in 1938. He later managed in the minor leagues, including the Toronto Maple Leafs, winning a pennant in 1943. He also served as a scout for teams like the Yankees, Athletics, and Orioles, where he is credited with discovering future Hall of Famers Jim Palmer and Dave McNally. He even had a role managing the Independence Yankees in 1948-1949, where a young Mickey Mantle began his professional career.

Burleigh Grimes was deservedly inducted into the National Baseball Hall of Fame in 1964 by the Veterans Committee. His election recognized his incredible durability and effectiveness over two distinct eras of baseball, his unique status as the last legal spitballer, and his enduring competitive fire. He left a profound and lasting legacy as one of baseball's most colorful and talented pitchers.

Dazzy Vance

Charles Arthur "Dazzy" Vance (1891-1961), affectionately known as "Dazzy" for his dazzling fastball, was a legendary figure in Major League Baseball. His remarkable 16-season career, spanning 21 years due to a unique path to stardom, left an indelible mark on the sport. It was primarily defined by his blazing fastball, unparalleled strikeout prowess, and an improbable late-career surge that culminated in his well-deserved induction into the National Baseball Hall of Fame.

Born on March 4, 1891, in Orient, Iowa, Vance spent most of his childhood in Nebraska, where he began playing semipro baseball. Standing 6 feet 2 inches tall and weighing 200 pounds, his physical presence matched his mighty arm. His early professional journey in the minor leagues, starting in 1912 at age 21, was plagued by persistent arm problems that often curtailed his promising starts. He had brief, unsuccessful stints in the Major Leagues with the Pittsburgh Pirates and New York Yankees in 1915, going 0-4 combined, and another two games with the Yankees in 1918, still without a win. For years, Vance bounced around minor league teams, from Columbus to Toledo, Memphis, Rochester, and Sacramento, unable to shake the arm troubles that consistently derailed his progress—a pivotal moment in his career, almost folkloric, occurred in 1920 while with the

New Orleans Pelicans. During a poker game, Vance reportedly injured his arm by banging it on a table, an incident some speculate may have paradoxically dislodged bone chips or cleared debris, leading to his arm suddenly feeling strong again. After this, his fortunes dramatically changed.

In 1921, at 30, Vance had a stellar 21-11 season for the New Orleans Pelicans, reigniting interest from Major League clubs. The Brooklyn Robins (who would later become the Dodgers) acquired his contract, reportedly for a nominal sum, with catcher Hank DeBerry being the primary target of the trade. Vance, a 31-year-old "rookie" in 1922, immediately justified the acquisition. He posted an 18-12 record and, crucially, led the National League with 134 strikeouts, the first of an unprecedented seven consecutive seasons (1922-1928) leading the league in that category. His fastball, which teammate Johnny Frederick famously quipped "could throw a cream puff through a battleship," became his signature weapon. Vance's most dominant individual season came in 1924 when he achieved pitching's coveted Triple Crown, leading the National League in wins (28), ERA (2.16), and strikeouts (262). He was awarded the National League Most Valuable Player Award for this exceptional performance, beating out Rogers Hornsby, who hit a staggering .424 that season. In 1924, he struck out more batters than the second and third-place pitchers combined and set a then-National League record by fanning 15 Chicago Cubs in a nine-inning game, later striking out 17 in a ten-inning game in 1925. He also pitched an immaculate inning on September 24, 1924, striking out three batters on nine pitches. On September 13, 1925, Vance threw a no-hitter against the Philadelphia Phillies. During his time with Brooklyn's "Daffiness Boys," Vance was also involved in the famous "three men on third" incident in 1926, adding to the team's colorful reputation. He consistently delivered 20-win seasons for the Robins throughout much of this period.

After a highly successful tenure with the Dodgers until 1932, Vance's career saw him move to the St. Louis Cardinals in 1933. He pitched for the Cincinnati Reds in 1934 before being waived back to the Cardinals. In 1934, as a member of the Cardinals' iconic "Gashouse Gang," Vance finally achieved his only World Series championship. Though a veteran by then, he made a key appearance, earning the win in Game 4 of the series. He also hit his seventh and final Major League home run that season, becoming the second-oldest pitcher to do so at 43 years and 6 months. As a reliever, he finished his remarkable career back with the Brooklyn Dodgers in 1935.

By his retirement in 1935, Dazzy Vance had amassed an impressive career record of 197 wins against 140 losses, with a 3.24 ERA and 2,045 strikeouts over 2,966.2 innings pitched. He completed 217 of his 349 starts and recorded 29 shutouts. His career statistics are particularly remarkable, considering he played only 33 innings of Major League Baseball before his age-31 breakout season. Vance also led the league in ERA thrice (1924, 1928, 1930).

After playing, Vance remained involved in baseball, primarily in Florida real estate, where he owned a hotel and thousands of acres of land, often regaling listeners with stories of his playing days. His memorable career was even immortalized in Ogden Nash's 1949 poem "Line-Up for Yesterday," which states: "V is for Vance, / The Dodgers' own Dazzy; / None of his rivals / Could throw as fast as he." Dazzy Vance was deservedly inducted into the National Baseball Hall of Fame in 1955, receiving 81.7% of the votes on his 16th ballot. His election recognized his incredible dominance during the 1920s, his unique journey to the big leagues, and his lasting legacy as one of baseball's greatest power pitchers.

Dazzy Vance Dodger Hall of Fame Pitcher-from Author's Dodger Museum Collection

Chapter Six
World War II and the New Era (1941-1946)

The autumn of 1941 should have been a triumphant moment for the Brooklyn Dodgers, a ball club teetering on the precipice of greatness. With a roster boasting sharp-eyed sluggers and hard-nosed pitchers, they stormed into the World Series, a long-awaited clash against the indomitable Yankees. Nevertheless, in that crisp October air, fate proved merciless. The Dodgers battled, clawed, and grasped for glory, yet the Yankees—so polished in their winning ways—proved unyielding. Brooklyn's dreams crumbled beneath the weight of their foe's experience, losing the series in five games. It was a bitter conclusion to a remarkable season, but in the coming years, the heartbreak of sport would pale beside the trials of a world at war. The Dodgers' 1941 season was nothing short of extraordinary. Finishing first in the National League with a 100-54 record, they led the league with 800 runs scored while allowing 581 runs. Their lineup was stacked with talent—Dolph Camilli, the slugging first baseman, powered his way to the National League MVP award with 34 home runs and 120 RBIs. Rookie sensation Pete Reiser electrified the diamond, leading the league in batting average (.343), slugging percentage (.558), and runs scored (117).

"Pistol" Pete Reiser literally ran through walls. Photo is from the Author's Dodger Museum Collection

On the mound, Whitlow Wyatt and Kirby Higbe each notched 22 wins, with Wyatt boasting a stingy 2.34 ERA. These performances underscored Brooklyn's dominance, but in the end, their brilliance in the regular season was overshadowed by their struggles in the World Series.

The 1941 World Series was a clash between Brooklyn and the Yankees, the perennial champions who had grown accustomed to October glory. The Yankees won in five games, sealing yet another championship. The series scores told a story of tight competition:

- Game 1: Yankees 3-2 Dodgers

- Game 2: Dodgers 3-2 Yankees

- Game 3: Yankees 2-1 Dodgers

- Game 4: Yankees 7-4 Dodgers

- Game 5: Yankees 3-1 Dodgers

Dixie Walker & "Ducky" Medwick 1941 Double Play Gum Card ACC # 330 from Author's Dodger Museum Collection

Despite standout performances, including Whitlow Wyatt's complete-game victory in Game 2, Brooklyn could not overcome the Yankees' relentless charge. Mickey Owen's infamous dropped third strike in Game 4 proved pivotal, allowing the Yankees to stage a dramatic rally. Joe Gordon was a thorn in Brooklyn's side, hitting .500 with one home run and 5 RBIs, while Charlie Keller added two homers and 6 RBIs. Brooklyn's bats faltered, posting a .182 team batting average, compared to the Yankees' .247.

With a 3.86 team ERA, the Dodgers struggled to contain their opponents, while the Yankees' 2.80 ERA kept Brooklyn in check.

Mickey Owen's passed ball likely cost Dodger's the 1941 World Series as it shifted the momentum of the Series. Autographed Photo from the Author's Dodger Museum Collection.

As the nation was thrust into World War II's unrelenting throes, baseball was tangled in the conflict's mighty grasp. Men who once graced Ebbets Field with their prowess now exchanged gloves for rifles, uniforms of flannel for fatigues. Among them was the fiery Leo Durocher, a manager whose cunning and brashness made him as much a force off the diamond as on it. The young and fleet-footed Pee Wee Reese, just beginning to carve his legend in the game's annals, answered his country's call. Whitlow Wyatt, Brooklyn's sturdy right-hander, whose fastball and guile had carried the Dodgers through the heat of competition, also donned the military's khaki. Reckless and fearless in his style of play, Pete Reiser saw his potential years in baseball curtailed by the war's demands.

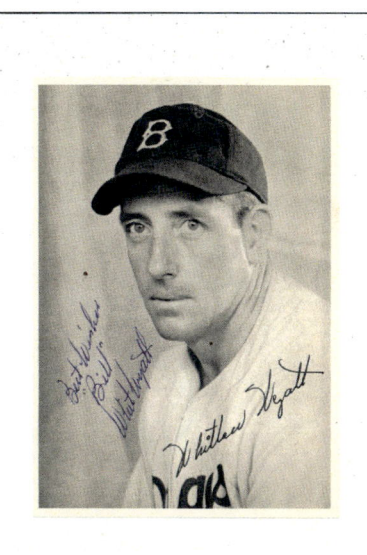

Whitlow Wyatt Autographed photo from Author's Dodger Museum Collection

While these men found themselves serving beyond the ballpark's boundaries, baseball became a crucial force of solace. In moments of respite, weary soldiers turned their gazes toward the game they once played as boys, a tether to the familiar in a world upended. Back home, in factories and shipyards, citizens found a reprieve from their tireless labors through radio broadcasts that carried the crack of the bat, the rise and fall of crowd roars, a momentary escape from the daunting realities of wartime sacrifice. Baseball, in all its simplicity, became a beacon—a reminder of a future beyond battlefields, where the only fights were for stolen bases and pennants.

Ebbets Field, the Dodgers' beloved home, adapted to the war effort in its way. In 1942, the Dodgers announced that any serviceman in uniform would be admitted to the ballpark free of charge. The stadium became a gathering place for baseball fans and those seeking a moment of normalcy amid the chaos of war. Even President Franklin D. Roosevelt made a campaign stop at Ebbets Field in 1944, delivering a speech in the rain, a testament to the ballpark's significance in American culture. With so many players departing for military service, the Dodgers had to rely on wartime replacements—players who might not have otherwise seen significant league action. Cookie Lavagetto, one of the first Dodgers to leave for service, was replaced by Arky Vaughan, acquired in a trade involving four players. Other replacements included Herman Franks, Joe Gallagher, Joe Hatten, Don Padgett, and Tommy Tatum, who filled the gaps left by departing stars. Like the country, the team had to adapt, relying on a mix of veterans, young prospects, and those deemed unfit for military duty.

The war left its mark on those who returned. Once a rising star, Pee Wee Reese returned to find his timing at the plate disrupted, his instincts dulled by years away from the game. Pete Reiser, whose reckless style had made him a fan favorite, returned with lingering injuries that would haunt him for the rest of his career.

"Gold Dust Twins" was moniker given to Reiser and Reese representing their Youth and Talent.

The emotional toll of war was evident in the clubhouse—some players carried the weight of their experiences in silence, while others found solace in the team's camaraderie.

Brooklyn's fan base remained steadfast through the war years. Even as star players left for service, attendance surged in 1945, with over 1,059,220 fans filling Ebbets Field, leading the National League. The Dodgers were more than a baseball team—they symbolized resilience, a source of pride for a borough that lived and breathed the game. Radio broadcasts became lifelines, carrying the voices of Red Barber and Connie Desmond into homes, bars, and factories, keeping Brooklyn connected to its beloved Dodgers.

Red Barber, Connie Desmond and Vin Scully from Author's Dodger Museum Collection

Opening Day in 1946 was a moment of catharsis. The war was over, and the Dodgers were back, stepping onto the field before a packed house at Ebbets Field. The crowd, buzzing with anticipation, roared as familiar faces returned to the diamond. The air was thick with the scent of hot dogs and cigars, the hum of conversation punctuated by the crack of the bat. It was more than just a game—a declaration that life had resumed in all its ordinary joys.

As 1946 dawned, the war finally ebbed, and the Dodgers stood ready to reclaim their place on the diamond. The team bore new faces alongside the returning heroes, each carrying the weight of years apart from the game they loved. The world had changed, and so too had baseball. No longer just a pastime, it had cemented itself as an enduring pillar of the American spirit—a symbol that had carried a nation through its darkest nights. For the Brooklyn Dodgers, the coming years would bring new battles, new heroes, and a long-awaited redemption. Still, their wartime role—one of sacrifice, resilience, and hope—would remain a chapter etched into history's ledger. From 1947 to 1957, it would prove to be a rollercoaster ride!

Autographed Picture from Author's Dodger Museum Collection.

Chapter Seven
Jackie Robinson and Breaking Barriers (1947)

From the very first moment that Jackie Robinson stepped onto the storied grounds of Ebbets Field, an electric charge coursed relentlessly through the very air—a portent of an era reborn, a clarion call destined to change the contours of America's pastime forever. In that incandescent debut, every measured stride and every determined glance served as a resounding denunciation of an age-old prejudice—a defiant rally against the oppressive chains of segregation. Like a comet blazing its brilliant trail across a midnight sky, Robinson's presence illuminated the field with the promise of a new dawn, heralding not only a transformation of baseball but also the birth of a social revolution that would shatter the long-held, unjust traditions of the past.

The game unfolded as a masterful overture—a vivid tapestry of sensory delights, emotional highs, and palpable tension. The sharp, defiant crack of bat on ball rang out like a sonnet to freedom amid a divided crowd, each note celebratory and poignant.

Branch Rickey signs Jackie Robinson to contract at Mechanics Bank Building, 215 Montague Street

The freshly cut grass exhaled the heady scent of hope and renewal, while the cool, whispering breeze caressed the scarred bleachers, carrying murmurs of a revolution that had long simmered beneath the surface. Every footfall on that hallowed green canvas became a brushstroke in an epic painting; every swing, every dive for a catch, every stolen base pulsed with the soaring promise of liberty and equality. Here, on that sacred field, the act of baseball transformed into a living metaphor for a nation teetering on the brink of profound change. Yet the impact of Robinson's arrival was not confined solely to the physical boundaries of Ebbets Field. Baseball—a sport steeped in tradition and long confined within the heavy hand of segregation—was abruptly elevated into a realm of vast social possibility and reinvention.

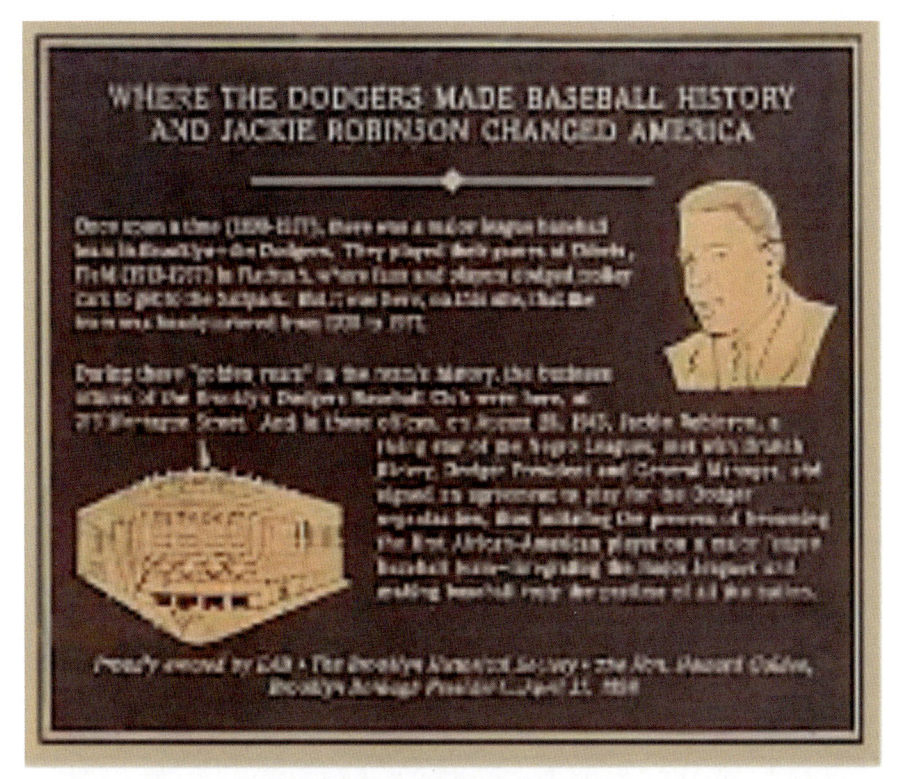

Commemorative Plaque

Once the mechanical domain of athletic routine, fly balls began to trace brilliant arcs against an endless azure sky, as if mapping out new constellations of hope. Gloves, erstwhile symbols of an exclusive tradition, now moved with determined defiance, catching the whizzing ball and the dreams and possibilities that fluttered in the summer air. With every play, the game transcended mere athletic competition. It emerged as a stirring symbol of a nation daring to dismantle injustice and embrace progress, collectively inching toward a future where racial barriers could finally crumble.

Leo Durocher welcomes Jackie Robinson

Amid this spectacle of on-field brilliance, the personal odyssey of Jackie Robinson unfolded as both a public spectacle and an intimate odyssey of struggle. Every dash between bases was not simply a mad rush towards victory but a courageous, heart-pounding sprint against the thunderous jeers and venomous vitriol that swirled in the humid air. The icy stares of opponents, laden with malice, and the deliberate isolation imposed by a society mired in prejudice, cut deeper than any blistering fastball. In those quiet interludes between innings, when the overwhelming roar of the crowd ebbed away to leave only an echoing silence, Robinson's heart bore the heavy weight of sacrifice. Hidden in the shadowed corners of locker rooms, unshed tears testified to the incessant cost of carrying his own dreams and the hopes of an entire nation yearning for justice, a burden borne with unwavering resolve and dignity.

Deep within the dugouts and locker rooms, a spectrum of raw, volatile emotions stirred among his teammates—a living mirror to a society undergoing monumental transition. Among these transformative exchanges, a singular moment emerged with celestial clarity: Pee Wee Reese's silent yet powerful embrace. In that fleeting, transcendent instance, Reese stepped forward and wrapped his arm around Robinson, an act of solidarity that spoke louder than any integrated proclamation could. Yet beyond that defining moment lay countless whispered conversations shared in the dim glow of late-night bus rides and the quiet intimacy of the clubhouse. Some teammates, long ensnared by the tendrils of ingrained bias, grappled silently with the brilliance of Robinson's play, their inner conflicts unfolding amid secret moments of introspection. Others, buoyed by the gentle warmth of his smile and the precision of every move, discovered in him not an aberration but a kindred spirit—a living testament to the idea that true greatness transcends both skin and circumstance. Every nod of understanding, every lingering look of admiration, and every unspoken word of support became a measured step along the arduous march toward complete racial unity, echoing the internal monologues of those who wondered if they too might someday evolve. Amid this maelstrom of public scrutiny and evolving team dynamics, another set of eyes and an indomitable heart bore silent witness to history in the making. Rachel Robinson, Jackie's steadfast wife, experienced that fateful day as an intimate odyssey interwoven with hope, trepidation, and fierce maternal love. Departing from the temporary shelter of their quarters at the McAlpin Hotel in Herald Square and accompanied by their infant son, Jackie Jr., she navigated the bustling, unpredictable streets of Brooklyn—a microcosm of the larger struggle unfolding on the field. Every hesitant step on crowded sidewalks, every frustrated bid to hail a cab amidst the city's ceaseless clamor, resonated with echoes of the obstacles that awaited her husband on the diamond. Yet beneath the palpable turbulence of the day lay an unshakable conviction—a profound, maternal certainty that Jackie's brave foray into baseball history would not merely transform the sport but also kindle a renaissance of justice for a divided nation. In the ambient murmur of cheering fans and the soft, hopeful whispers of strangers along the avenue, Rachel perceived both the crushing burden of what was at stake and the luminous promise of change, inspiring her internal resolve in moments of quiet reflection.

In stark contrast to this swelling chorus of hope and unity, the bitter face of entrenched bigotry loomed: the hateful figure of Ben Chapman, the Philadelphia Phillies manager known for his venomous diatribes and racist invectives, who loomed like a specter from an unrepentant past. Chapman, with a tongue honed on rancor and a heart mired in prejudice, unleashed a relentless barrage of racial slurs—words aimed squarely at discrediting Robinson's historic moment. His bitter abuse, intended to erode the emerging spirit of unity, instead magnified the enormity of the struggle, serving as a raw reminder that change would not come without sacrifice. In the seething furnace of Chapman's vitriol, the purity and defiance of Robinson's achievements shone brighter still, galvanizing both onlookers and allies alike and reinforcing the moral imperative to push forward for a just tomorrow.

Jackie Robinson "Rattles" the opposition. He stole home 19 times out of 31 attempts, and once in the World Series. Picture colorized by the author.

At the helm of this epochal transformation stood Branch Rickey, the visionary strategist and moral architect whose daring gamble on integration would forever revolutionize American baseball. With a mind as incisive as the sharpest pitch and a heart set ablaze by idealism, Rickey recognized in Robinson not merely a prodigious athlete, but a luminous beacon destined to lead America toward fairness and unity. In the hushed corridors of Brooklyn's front offices, where meticulous calculation met enduring moral conviction, Rickey meticulously devised plans that far surpassed the conventional limits of a baseball contract. His design was a covenant—a solemn pledge that a man of unyielding character, tempered by dignified restraint, could upend the entrenched forces of hate and prejudice. Rickey's vision, a seamless blend of strategic brilliance and soulful appeal to America's better angels, resonated deeply with every member of the Dodgers organization, its impact rippling outward into the very fabric of society and sowing seeds of hope that would flourish for generations.

Other stalwarts emerged as indispensable heralds of progress within that same revolutionary milieu. Don Newcombe and Roy Campanella, forging their courageous paths within the newly integrated ranks, were busy rewriting the very playbook of possibility. Even as Robinson mesmerized audiences with his unparalleled brilliance at Ebbets Field and with the Montreal Royals, Newcombe and Campanella were penning separate chapters in the grand saga of change with the Nashua Dodgers—the first integrated affiliated team in the United States. On modest ballfields, nurtured by the guidance of forward-thinking mentors like a young Walter Alston, Newcombe's masterful command on the mound and Campanella's unwavering leadership behind the plate combined in a stirring symphony of triumph over deep-seated prejudice. Their excellence, manifest amid the fervor of jubilant crowds and the steady pulse of a transforming game, declared with quiet authority that talent and unwavering determination could outshine even the most entrenched dictates of division.

Beyond the confines of the diamond, the magnitude of that historic day reverberated throughout every facet of American life. Across the nation, newspapers clattered on typewriters as eloquent penmen captured the electrifying details of Robinson's debut, crafting headlines that hailed him as the harbinger of moral renewal and social rebirth. Radio broadcasters' voices imbued with the passion and cadence of revered prophets recited his feats with an intensity that transformed each airwave into a moving sermon of hope. The ambient roar of the stands, intermingled with the hushed, reverent whispers that followed every pivotal play, created a national tapestry—a living chronicle affirming that history was being rewritten with every brave act of defiance. In an added echo of timeless change, modern voices have carried forward the legacy of that transformative day with remarkable clarity. Today's athletes, many of whom openly champion social justice and challenge inequality on and off the field, stand on the shoulders of these pioneering giants. Contemporary protests, digital campaigns, and public statements of solidarity have become the modern continuation of the struggle once waged on baseball diamonds. Whether it is the resounding clamor of social media movements or the resolute stands taken by sports figures in boardrooms and press conferences, the spirit of 1947 endures, igniting change and inspiring a new generation to shatter the remnants of discrimination with the same fervor that once echoed through Ebbets Field.

Roy Campanella, Don Newcombe and Jackie Robinson

Deep in the hearts of those who witnessed the unfolding drama—both on the field and in the quiet recesses of their souls—there emerged intimate reflections and internal monologues that testified to the enormity of the moment. Teammates recalled in private chatter how each stolen base was intertwined with personal doubts and secret revelations; each play was an internal conquest over long-held fears. In those moments, the whispers of a better world spoke softly, urging every individual to courageously embrace change and acknowledge that the path to justice is as much an internal battle as an external triumph.

Historical context further underscores the epic nature of that day. As 1947 marked a turning point in sports and a pivotal moment in the broader civil rights movement, the echoes of Robinson's triumph resonated with other struggles for equality across America. The nation, still emerging from the shadows of World War II and grappling with its imperfections, found in his bold stance a symbol of hope that extended far beyond the baseball diamond. His debut became interwoven with the aspirations of countless Americans who longed for a future unfettered by the restraints of an outdated, segregated past.

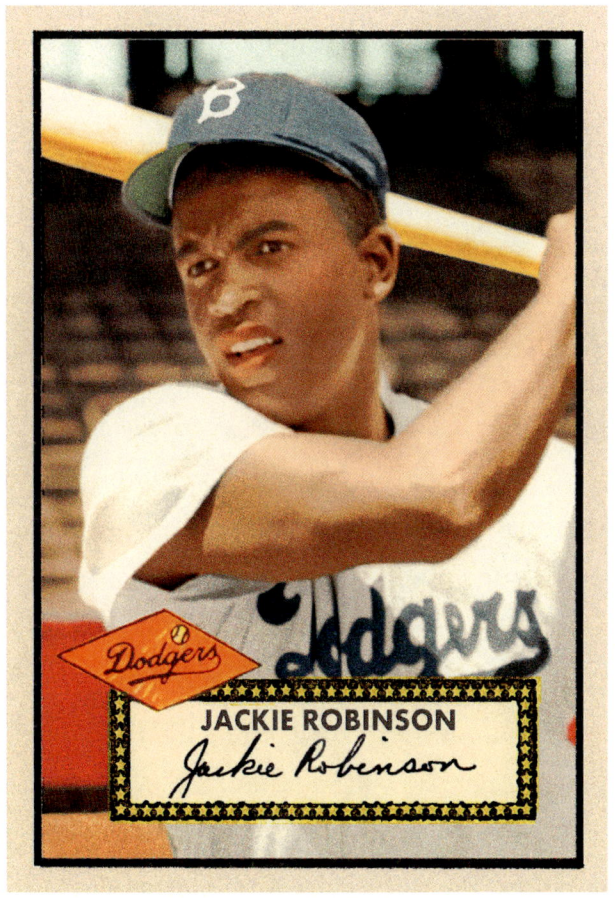

Alternate version of Jackie Robinson 1952 Topps card

As the season advanced, the intertwined destinies of these trailblazing figures—Robinson, his steadfast teammates, Branch Rickey, Don Newcombe, Roy Campanella, and even those representing bitter opposition like Ben Chapman—wove together an intricate tapestry that transcended the familiar confines of a sports game to embed its luminous narrative into the heart of the nation. In long, reflective bus rides beneath towering stadium lights and during quiet, contemplative moments following a hard-fought contest, players and spectators alike recounted with heartfelt candor the mix of trepidation, hope, and profound transformation that swept over them. Every nod of understanding, every shared smile, and every fleeting touch of genuine camaraderie testified that the pursuit of equality is not a solitary struggle but a collective odyssey—a journey demanding unwavering courage, deep empathy, and the persistent breaking of chains that have long divided us.

Today, the legacy of Jackie Robinson burns with the unyielding brilliance of the midday sun—a living, breathing beacon lighting the path for every generation that follows. His steadfast insistence on demanding inalienable respect, his unwavering commitment to human dignity, and his quiet, relentless defiance in the face of towering adversity continue to resonate with as much force now as in that historic summer of 1947. Modern echoes of his courage reverberate in every daring play on the diamond, every uncompromising stance against systemic injustice, and every public celebration that honors the vibrant, multifaceted tapestry of human diversity. In the intricate interplay between athletic prowess and enduring social progress,

Robinson's memory calls upon us all to confront inequality wherever it rears its head and affirm every individual's timeless, shared worth.

In the enduring light of that transformative day at Ebbets Field, Jackie Robinson's journey intensifies the call for change and stands as a towering monument to the power of unified courage. Their storied legacy, indelibly etched in the annals of sports history and memorialized in the hearts of all who yearn for justice, compels us to recognize that the struggle for equality is perpetual, that the seeds of progress are sown in the soil of relentless determination, and that every act of brave defiance holds the promise of ushering in a more inclusive, compassionate world. This epic narrative is not simply a recollection of past triumphs; it is a vibrant, evolving call to persist amid adversity, to resolutely challenge injustice at every turn, and to wholeheartedly embrace our shared humanity with the passion and verve of a nation reborn.

In the spirit of Grantland Rice—a master storyteller who elevated sport into myth and legend—this chronicle sings not only of the heroic exploits upon the baseball diamond but also of an enduring quest for justice that spans generations. It reminds us that the courage to break barriers, then and now, is the timeless spark that ignites the fires of transformation, urging every new generation to stride boldly into a future resplendent with hope, enriched by diversity, and boundless in possibility.

ALLEN SCHERY

Walter O'Malley, Rachel Robinson, and Jackie Robinson celebrate.

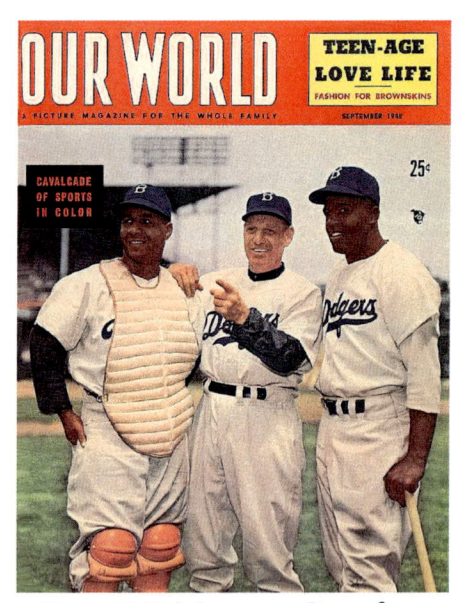

Rare 1948 Magazine Cover from Author's Dodger Museum Collection

Chapter Eight
Passing the Baton

In the pantheon of baseball history, where the sacred echoes of cheering multitudes mingle with the timeless murmurs of legends past, few figures shine with as incandescent a brilliance-or as labyrinthine a complexity as Walter O'Malley. More than a conventional sports executive, O'Malley emerged as a consummate businessman whose illustrious career in engineering, construction, and law forged an impenetrable foundation for one of the most transformative eras ever witnessed in America's beloved pastime. His storied journey toward becoming the primary owner of the Brooklyn Dodgers in the turbulent 1940s and beyond unfolds as a saga of strategic capitalization, innovative ingenuity, and an audacious long-term vision that reimagined the very essence of baseball. In those heady days, when the beleaguered Dodgers teetered on the brink of insolvency—ensnared by a staggering debt exceeding $700,000 owed to the venerable Brooklyn Trust Company—O'Malley, already battle-hardened by years of public works and infrastructural marvels, embarked upon a meticulously calculated path to sports ownership. Aligning himself with an illustrious consortium of investors, including the indomitable Branch Rickey—whose pioneering innovations would soon shatter the old paradigms of the game—and a cadre of key financiers whose deep reservoirs of capital and unassailable credibility lent rare gravitas to his bold ambition, he began the painstaking process of acquiring shares in the time-honored franchise. At the heart of this financial renaissance stood the formidable George V. McLaughlin, a powerful civic luminary whose dual roles as Brooklyn's Police Commissioner and President of the bank that steadied the Dodgers brought an aura of resolute stability and pragmatic wisdom to the unfolding narrative. In the waning days of the 1930s, as financial misfortunes and internal feuds between the McKeever interests and the Ebbets heirs threatened to dismember the soul of the team, McLaughlin's intervention—pressuring the discordant factions to embrace the steady hand of capable leadership—ushered in the appointment of a young Walter O'Malley as legal counsel. Under McLaughlin's astute guidance, the once beleaguered organization embarked on a remarkable journey of financial restructuring, borrowing a modest $200,000 even as the brilliant general manager Larry MacPhail skillfully parried mounting debts down to an impressive $350,000 while preserving a vital reserve of $150,000. This remarkable turnaround set the stage for O'Malley's inexorable deepening involvement—a process marked by his acquisition of a pivotal 25% stake in the Dodgers alongside visionary figures such as Rickey, the erudite insurance executive Andrew Schmitz, and John L. Smith, a distinguished Pfizer president and Chairman of the Board introduced to the team's labyrinthine financial dealings through McLaughlin's sagacious influence. Smith, whose calming presence and deft mediation between the towering personalities of Rickey and O'Malley stabilized a tempestuous power struggle and whose relentless push to consolidate ownership—facilitated through acquiring shares from the embattled McKeever family in 1944 and then the venerable Ebbets estate in 1945.

BROOKLYN DODGERS AT EBBETS FIELD 1913-1957

Standing (l-r) Dodger Vice President Walter O'Malley, Borough President John Cashmore, Judge Henry Ughetta, member Dodger Board of Directors. Sitting (l-r) Dodger President Branch Rickey, Admiral Edwin Peck, Commanding Officer of Vero Beach Naval Air Base, John L. Smith, Dodger stockholder

This ensured the future integrity of the franchise, eventually had his promising influence curtailed by a tragic diagnosis of lung cancer in early 1950, his eventual passing on a fateful July day catalyzing a final transfer of his shares to O'Malley via his widow, Mary Louise Smith, in January 1958.

Walter O'Malley and Mary Louise Smith widow of John L. Smith

The formidable financial acumen that propelled O'Malley's rise was not the artifact of mere serendipity but the cumulative result of hard-won success in the demanding arenas of engineering and public works contracting—ventures as monumental as the extensive geological investigations and the visionary development of infrastructure like New York City's Midtown Tunnel—that imbued him with an unerring ability to perceive long-term investment opportunities and sustainable growth. With this rare blend of resource and insight, he transformed a shared stake in a cherished institution into undisputed control over a major league franchise, his every share acquisition and every nuanced negotiation interwoven into a grand tapestry of legacy that extended far beyond the confines of the ballpark. No industry titan, however, ever rises in splendid isolation; O'Malley's crowning achievement was enriched by a constellation of illustrious partners whose distinct personalities and purpose-driven ideals lent the endeavor its vibrant, multifaceted brilliance. Among these, Branch Rickey emerged not solely as an astute financial backer but as a visionary executive whose groundbreaking ideas—foremost among them the historic breaking of the color barrier—would leave an indelible mark on modern baseball, while John L. Smith, born Johann Schmitz and reformed by the pressures of anti-German sentiment in a postwar America, contributed an unwavering blend of financial acumen and cultural resilience, further solidified by his deep connections within the inner circles of business power. (Andrew and Johann Schmitz were relatives) Complementing these forces was the singular, almost mythic, presence of Steve McKeever—a man renowned both for his stern, almost ascetic demeanor and his devout Catholic principles; a man whose peculiar yet endearing fondness for drinking milk at games, rather than succumbing to the typical allure of alcohol, set him apart in a world of hardened executives, and whose unyielding belief in the sanctity of marriage only served to heighten the simmering tensions that erupted when Charles Ebbets' daughter, Genevieve Ebbets Gilleaudeau, faced the wrenching passage of divorce, thereby deepening the longstanding rifts between the McKeever loyalists and the Ebbets heirs. These palpable fissures, mirrored in the physical distances between adversarial factions during tense ownership meetings, underscored the turbulent yet transformative nature of the Dodgers' internal dynamics. The tempest grew even more poignant with McKeever's untimely death in March 1938—a tragic moment that further complicated the intricate tapestry of ownership, as his significant 50% stake passed into the care of his beloved daughter, Elizabeth Marie "Dearie" Mulvey, whose steadfast husband, James Mulvey, continued to play an influential role in the team's business affairs until the decisive moment in 1950, when Walter O'Malley assumed his preeminent position. Even as the Mulvey family retained a lingering 25% minority share until Dearie's passing in 1968, their eventual absorption into O'Malley's expanding empire by 1975, nearly two decades after the monumental relocation to Los Angeles, firmly underscored the unassailable power of his vision.

Ultimately, the extraordinary narrative of Walter O'Malley—spanning the disciplined realms of engineering and legal strategy to the incandescent arenas of sports management—stands as a masterclass in interdisciplinary genius and audacious leadership. His transformative decisions, especially the bold and often contentious relocation of the Dodgers to the glimmering expanses of Los Angeles, reverberated like a symphonic crescendo through the corridors of modern baseball economics, dismantling old paradigms and recasting the game in the brilliant light of innovation. In the final analysis, O'Malley's legacy transcends mere financial maneuvering or ownership consolidation; it is a fundamental and resplendent reshaping of the baseball industry, a timeless testament to the power of bold leadership and diverse expertise to change the very fabric of the game for generations to come.

BROOKLYN DODGERS AT EBBETS FIELD 1913-1957

Elizabeth Marie "Dearie" McKeever Mulvey, and her husband, James Mulvey in later years.

Chapter Nine
Larry MacPhail and the Transformation of the Brooklyn Dodgers (1938-1942)

In the late 1930s, the Brooklyn Dodgers were a franchise in turmoil. The team had long struggled with mediocrity, failing to impact the National League standings significantly. Fans remained loyal, but frustration was growing. The club desperately needed a visionary leader who could modernize operations, energize the fan base, and construct a winning team. Enter Larry MacPhail, a brash, innovative executive known for shaking the baseball world.

MacPhail had previously demonstrated his ability to revolutionize a ball club with the Cincinnati Reds, where he introduced night baseball and dramatically improved revenue and attendance. In 1938, the Dodgers hired him to overhaul their struggling organization. Over the next four years, MacPhail reshaped not only the Dodgers but also the future of baseball itself. However, behind his brilliant mind lay a tumultuous personal life, often exacerbated by his drinking habits, which made his leadership both electrifying and volatile.

Larry MacPhail was fearless in his approach to change. He wasted no time implementing new ideas, introducing innovations that would ultimately become staples of Major League Baseball. One of his most impactful decisions was bringing night baseball to Brooklyn. While some baseball purists viewed evening games as a novelty, MacPhail recognized their potential to attract larger crowds. He spearheaded the lights installation at Ebbets Field, allowing games to be played after sunset. On June 15, 1938, the Dodgers played their first night game, and the results were electric; the stands were filled with fans who otherwise might not have been able to attend daytime contests. Attendance surged, revenue increased, and soon other teams followed Brooklyn's lead. Today, night games are the norm, but in the late 1930s, MacPhail's decision was bold and groundbreaking.

Another area where MacPhail was ahead of his time was radio broadcasts. He understood that allowing fans to listen to games on the radio could broaden the team's reach and create lifelong supporters. While some baseball executives feared radio would hurt ticket sales, MacPhail embraced the medium. Under his leadership, the Dodgers expanded their radio presence, ensuring that Brooklyn baseball could be heard across the region. This decision solidified the Dodgers' reputation as one of the most accessible and fan-friendly franchises.

MacPhail wasn't just a visionary but also a shrewd talent evaluator who made bold roster moves to improve the Dodgers. He aggressively reshaped the team during his tenure, bringing in smart acquisitions and developing a competitive roster. In 1941, MacPhail's efforts culminated in the Dodgers winning their first National League pennant since 1920. His emphasis on building a strong roster paid off, proving that his aggressive strategies weren't just about spectacle—they were about winning.

Larry MacPhail was part genius and part bombastic.

While MacPhail was changing the landscape of baseball, his personal life was marked by heavy drinking and unpredictable behavior. His love for alcohol often brought out his brash, confrontational personality, leading to explosive outbursts, heated arguments, and impulsive decisions. Some within the Dodgers organization struggled to manage his erratic temperament, as his drinking would sometimes escalate into rage-fueled confrontations with players, executives, and reporters. Yet, despite these challenges, MacPhail's brilliance and innovations outweighed his flaws, keeping him firmly in control of the team until the pressures of leadership and personal demons began to take their toll.

The 1941 season marked a significant milestone for the Dodgers under MacPhail. Brooklyn finished the season 100-54, capturing the National League pennant with strong pitching, power hitting, and aggressive strategy. Brooklyn advanced to the World Series, facing off against the powerhouse New York Yankees. Though the Dodgers fought hard, they lost the series in five games, a bitter pill for MacPhail to swallow. The loss was excruciating because of the infamous passed ball incident in Game 4. With the game tied, Dodgers catcher Mickey Owen mishandled a third strike, allowing Yankee Tommy Henrich to reach base instead of ending the inning. The Yankees rallied and won the game, swinging the momentum their way.

MacPhail was devastated—not just as an executive, but as an emotionally invested leader. The loss seemed to deepen his frustration with certain game elements, and his behavior became increasingly erratic in the following months. MacPhail was a brilliant baseball mind, but he was also volatile. He was known for his fiery temper, drinking habits, and conflicts with fellow executives.

One of the most significant tensions in baseball at the time existed between Larry MacPhail and Branch Rickey. Rickey, a calculating strategist, had very different management philosophies from MacPhail. Their clashes led to internal disputes within the Dodgers organization. While Rickey was known for his reserved, intellectual approach, MacPhail was bombastic, emotional, and impulsive. These personality differences made collaboration difficult, and eventually, MacPhail's days in Brooklyn became numbered.

Larry MacPhail in a calmer more pensive moment.

Despite their differences, both men were transformative figures in baseball. MacPhail's boldness and willingness to take risks contrasted sharply with Rickey's methodical and strategic mindset. Rickey's later achievements, including the signing of Jackie Robinson, were built upon the foundation of modernization and innovation that MacPhail had established.

By September 1942, MacPhail made an unexpected announcement—he was leaving baseball to serve in the United States Army during World War II. While the departure shocked many, MacPhail had always viewed himself as patriotic and duty driven. His departure marked the end of one of the most dramatic and transformative eras in the Brooklyn Dodgers' history. MacPhail's resignation wasn't just about military service but also stemmed from his burnout and increasing frustrations with the baseball establishment. Many speculate that his drinking and emotional volatility played a role in his sudden decision to leave the game.

MacPhail's tenure with the Dodgers was brief, but his impact was profound. His innovations, including night games, radio broadcasts, and aggressive roster-building strategies, became permanent fixtures in professional baseball. Following MacPhail's departure, Branch Rickey took over and continued building upon the foundation he had helped lay. Rickey later revolutionized baseball by signing Jackie Robinson in 1947, but much of the Dodgers' organizational modernization had already been set in motion by MacPhail.

MacPhail later worked with the New York Yankees, where his drinking led to infamous outbursts, including punching a friend at the 1947 World Series victory celebration. Despite his struggles, his bold leadership earned him Hall of Fame recognition, cementing his place among the sport's most influential executives.

Larry MacPhail was far more than a baseball executive—he was a trailblazer, an innovator, and a fiery personality who reshaped the game. His boldness, vision, and willingness to challenge convention helped turn the Brooklyn Dodgers from an ordinary franchise into a contender. Though his time in Brooklyn was tumultuous, his legacy endures. MacPhail's risk-taking and leadership helped shape baseball as we know it today.

ALLEN SCHERY

Walter O'Malley, who later became the Dodgers' owner, built upon many of MacPhail's innovations when shaping the franchise's future. O'Malley's strategic vision and business acumen helped transform the Dodgers into one of baseball's most successful and iconic teams. While O'Malley's contributions were distinct, the foundation laid by MacPhail's bold leadership and willingness to challenge convention played a crucial role in the team's evolution.

Chapter Ten
The Tempestuous Leo Durocher

Leo Durocher began his professional baseball career as an infielder, known more for his defensive prowess than his hitting ability. He made his Major League debut with the New York Yankees in 1925, but his time with the team was brief, and he was traded to the Cincinnati Reds in 1930. After several seasons in Cincinnati, he moved to the St. Louis Cardinals in 1933, where he became a key member of the famed "Gashouse Gang" that won the 1934 World Series. Durocher was known for his fiery personality even as a player, often clashing with opponents and umpires while maintaining a reputation as a strong leader. In 1938, he joined the Brooklyn Dodgers, serving as a player and team captain before transitioning into a managerial role in 1939. Over his playing career, Durocher compiled a .247 batting average, 24 home runs, and 567 RBIs, but his most significant contributions came in his leadership and defensive skills. His transition from player to manager marked the beginning of a long and influential career in baseball, where his aggressive style and sharp baseball mind would leave a lasting impact on the sport.

Leo Durocher was with all New York Teams

Durocher quickly established himself as a fiery and strategic leader upon taking over as Brooklyn's manager in 1939. His first full season at the helm in 1940 saw the Dodgers improve to a 79-75 record, signaling a shift in the team's competitiveness. By 1941, Durocher had transformed Brooklyn into a legitimate contender, leading the team to a National League pennant with a 100-54 record, their first World Series appearance since 1920. Though they ultimately lost to the Yankees in five games, the Dodgers had established themselves as a force in the National League. Over the next few years, Durocher continued to push the team forward, finishing second in 1942 with 104 wins but falling just short of the pennant behind the Cardinals. His leadership emphasized aggressive play, sharp defense, and a vocal clubhouse presence that often put him at odds with umpires and league officials. One of his most notable conflicts was with Dodgers president Larry MacPhail, a strong-willed executive known for his innovations and volatile temperament. Their relationship was marked by frequent clashes, including an incident in 1941 when MacPhail believed Durocher had deliberately ordered a train conductor to bypass a scheduled stop where MacPhail had planned a champagne celebration for the team's pennant victory. Durocher denied involvement, but MacPhail remained convinced it was an intentional snub. Their tensions escalated further when MacPhail accused Durocher of gambling after he won a bingo prize at a pre-spring training event, leading to repeated threats of dismissal that MacPhail never carried out. However, their feud broke in 1947 when Durocher publicly criticized MacPhail for allegedly entertaining gamblers in his box during spring training. This charge contributed to Durocher's season-long suspension by Commissioner Happy Chandler.

Leo Durocher and Laraine Day

Durocher's 1947 suspension was one of the most controversial moments in baseball history. Chandler cited Durocher's associations with gamblers, his gambling debts, and his tumultuous personal life as reasons for the suspension. The decision was met with outrage from Dodgers fans, as Durocher had been instrumental in shaping the team's competitive identity. During Jackie Robinson's historic debut season, his absence was particularly significant, as Durocher had been a vocal supporter of Robinson's inclusion on the team. Despite his suspension, the Dodgers won the National League pennant under interim manager Burt Shotton, though they ultimately lost to the Yankees in the World Series. The suspension marked a turning point in Durocher's career, reinforcing his reputation as one of baseball's most controversial figures.

Durocher returned to manage the team in 1948. Still, midseason, he made a shocking departure, leaving Brooklyn after compiling a 40-37 record that year to take over as manager for the rival New York Giants. His Dodgers career ended with a managerial record of 738 wins and 565 losses, including two National League pennants. Though controversy and clashes with league officials marked his tenure, his impact on the Dodgers was undeniable, helping shape the franchise into a perennial contender. His departure to the Giants was met with outrage from Brooklyn fans, but his managerial success continued as he later led the Giants to a World Series championship in 1954.

Burt Shotton with Dan Bankhead

In the 1960s, Durocher returned to the Dodgers as a coach from 1961 to 1964, working under manager Walter Alston. His presence in the dugout brought his signature fiery personality and deep baseball knowledge to a new generation of Dodgers players. During this period, he contributed to the team's success, including their 1963 World Series victory. Though he was no longer the manager, his impact on the Dodgers remained significant, as he continued to shape the team's competitive spirit and strategic approach to the game. His time as a coach further cemented his legacy as one of baseball's most influential figures, ensuring that his contributions to the Dodgers extended well beyond his managerial years.

After his time with the Dodgers, Durocher returned to managing in 1966 when the Chicago Cubs hired him. The Cubs had been struggling for decades, but under Durocher's leadership, they showed significant improvement. After finishing tenth in his first season, the Cubs climbed to third place in 1967 and 1968. In 1969, the Cubs were in first place for most of the season and were expected to win the pennant, but they collapsed down the stretch and finished second to the New York Mets. Durocher faced criticism for his team handling; by the early 1970s, he had lost control of the clubhouse, with some players openly rebelling against his autocratic style. In August 1972, Durocher replaced Harry Walker as manager of the Houston Astros, becoming one of the few managers to lead two National League teams in a single season. He remained with the Astros through 1973 before stepping down, citing health reasons. By the end of his managerial career, Durocher had amassed 2,008 wins, ranking among the most successful managers in baseball history. Though he was often embroiled in controversy, his strategic brilliance and relentless drive to win left an indelible mark on the game. He was posthumously inducted into the Baseball Hall of Fame in 1994, cementing his legacy as one of baseball's most influential figures.

Newspaper says it all!

Chapter Eleven
Rickey and O'Malley

Rickey had long sensed the winds of change. "The greatest untapped resource in the history of America is its young men," he once proclaimed—his voice imbued with conviction as he believed that every player, irrespective of race or background, deserved a chance to shape the game. His philosophy was rooted in scouting, development, and audacious social pioneering. However, even as he recognized the opportunity, he was acutely aware that exercising control was an entirely different matter, especially as financial pressures mounted. As he prepared to move on by selling his 25 percent stake in the team, he expected external investors to share his vision, hoping his legacy of progress and baseball ingenuity would endure untarnished.

Meanwhile, Walter O'Malley, ever the shrewd strategist and a man driven by a singular vision of modern corporate management for baseball, realized that this was his moment to take over control. By exercising his preemptive rights, he moved decisively, buying Rickey's shares and aligning with Mrs. John L. Smith, thus asserting command over 75 percent of the club's stock. On September 22, 1950, when Rickey formally approached O'Malley with a potential outside offer, he was offered exactly $346,666.66 for his shares—a figure matching what he, O'Malley, and Smith had originally paid in the mid-1940s. While substantial, this amount was far from the $1 million price tag Rickey had envisioned—a value he believed truly reflected the franchise's burgeoning worth and his invaluable contributions to its success and societal impact. The news broke in the Brooklyn Eagle the next day, and a public declaration of the seismic shift was underway. O'Malley promptly announced his intent to match the bid, securing his contractual right to acquire Rickey's stake and solidifying his position as the dominant force in the Dodgers' future. The power dynamic had irrevocably shifted, marking not just a change in ownership but a profound shift in the team's governance, setting the stage for O'Malley's undisputed reign.

"As the landscape of baseball evolved, Jackie Robinson remained steadfast in his commitment to progress and fairness. In his Look magazine article, A Kentucky Colonel Kept Me In Baseball, Part II, Robinson reflected on the remarkable shift in the sport. 'I never hesitate to speak up about anything on my mind,' he wrote. So he posed a direct question to Dodger president Walter O'Malley, asking whether the team would ever set a limit on the number of Black players. O'Malley responded unwavering: The Dodgers would field nine Black players if they were the best. This statement underscored the club's commitment to merit-based inclusion, which had come a long way since Robinson's historic signing. Last summer, when five Black players appeared in Brooklyn's lineup, the lack of public reaction spoke volumes. A franchise that had once sparked national uproar with the signing of a single Black player had now integrated so thoroughly that it scarcely drew comment. Robinson could not help but think that maybe democracy in the U.S.A. is doing better now than many people are willing to believe."

Walter O'Malley and Branch Rickey

Robinson knew that such progress had required bold leadership from the start. Branch Rickey, the visionary behind baseball's racial integration, had emphasized that ownership was the first major hurdle in breaking the color line. Reflecting on the early resistance, Rickey noted in The American Diamond that in St. Louis, in the 1940s, even Black spectators were barred from sitting in the grandstand. Brooklyn's ownership, however, had embraced change, approving the employment of Black players in professional baseball, a landmark decision that would forever alter the sport.

Rickey had also acknowledged the essential support he needed to make Robinson's historic signing a reality. In the 1965 film The Old Ball Game, he admitted that without the backing of fellow owners—including O'Malley, John L. Smith, and James and Dearie Mulvey—Robinson's groundbreaking entry into Major League Baseball might never have happened. The Brooklyn Baseball Club's Board of Directors had stood firmly behind this transformative move, setting the stage for a new era.

Years later, Robinson watched the game's continuing transformation with pride and unease. He had helped reshape baseball, but the world kept moving, ushering in new challenges. His guiding principle—"A life is not important except in the impact it has on other lives"—resonated ever more deeply as he weighed the shifting tides between honoring his legacy and embracing the future.

Meanwhile, Walter O'Malley pressed forward with his vision, determined to propel baseball into the modern age. The venture entwined Hollywood's glamour with the sport's raw passion. O'Malley's bold installment strategies and innovative business maneuvers would not only redefine the economics of baseball but also set the stage for the sport's expansion into new markets and realms of media. While Rickey retreated to Pittsburgh hoping to fashion a new order, the foundational alterations he had wrought continued to underpin the game, imprinting on every prospect and every barrier that was eventually shattered.

In those final days of Rickey's tenure, the air at Ebbets Field carried the scent of roasted peanuts and smoldering cigars, the hum of a restless crowd blending with the distant clatter of subways beneath Brooklyn's busy streets. Wooden seats groaned under shifting bodies while fervent vendors called out their orders, and the sharp crack of a bat echoed across the diamond like a shot fired into history. In the glow of a golden afternoon, Jackie Robinson dug his cleats deep into the dust, the weight of expectation as palpable as the humid heat of a late Brooklyn summer. His every move on the field was a testament to the quiet revolution Rickey had set in motion, a testament to courage and change, oblivious to the high-stakes chess match unfolding behind closed doors. In the executive offices, far removed from the jubilant chaos of the field, a different kind of battle was taking shape—a struggle of contracts, control, and the very leadership of baseball itself, a future being reshaped with every stroke of a pen that sealed Rickey's exit and ushered in a more business-centric approach.

Branch Rickey had "worldly" ideas

In the interim, as complex financial negotiations echoed through boardrooms, and the crowd's roar reverberated on the field, Rickey began packing his considerable legacy into boxes. With a heavy heart, he lingered at the threshold of his office, a place imbued with years of tireless dedication. In this space, the blueprints for the Dodgers' groundbreaking farm system and the meticulous refinement of a champion talent pipeline were etched into every scarred surface. Memories of long nights spent sifting through scouting reports, poring over player statistics, and intense debates over strategy filled his thoughts, alongside recollections of players once deemed destined to revolutionize the game. It was his life's work, carefully boxed away. Outside, Ebbets Field stood as a quiet cathedral of baseball, its atmosphere steeped in history and the triumph of breaking barriers—a legacy immortalized by Robinson's debut steps and the promise of a more inclusive future that now seemed to stretch uncertainly into the horizon, under new stewardship, a future whose course O'Malley alone would now chart a common sense business approach.

Nevertheless, the unfolding drama was not confined to sentimental farewells; the financial complexities of the transfer continued to deepen. Three weeks later, in mid-October 1950, O'Malley and Mrs. Smith announced their intent to split Rickey's shares. This move would drastically alter the Dodgers' destiny by cementing O'Malley's ultimate control. On November 1, 1950, O'Malley formally accepted the buyout, anticipating a shared financial burden. However, the situation's complexity deepened when, on November 20, 1950, Mrs. Smith abruptly withdrew from the agreement. This unforeseen decision left O'Malley solely responsible for the entire purchase, placing immense financial strain on him, especially considering he had recently borrowed heavily to buy out other co-owners.

O'Malley agreed on November 24 to alleviate this substantial burden by adopting an intricate installment plan reminiscent of Rickey's previous negotiation with real estate magnate William Zeckendorf. This strategy stipulated a $175,000 down payment due by December 5, 1950, followed by an additional $125,000 due by March 1, 1951. The remaining $750,000 was to be spread over ten annual installments starting in 1952, with the Dodgers' future earnings explicitly set to finance these payments. This complex financial maneuver demonstrated not only O'Malley's audacious vision but also his unwavering determination to assume complete control of the team's future, solidifying his singular authority as the team's primary owner, poised to steer the franchise in a new, more commercially driven direction.

Amid the shifting balance of power and these intricate negotiations, Jackie Robinson, whose trailblazing career had long symbolized hope and progress, watched as the landscape of baseball transformed around him. Once the embodiment of Rickey's revolutionary ideals, Robinson now sensed that the grand experiment of the Dodgers was evolving without his mentor's direct influence. The pioneering spirit that had brought him to the major leagues was yielding to the inexorable pressures of modern business. Though he had always looked ahead, his heart ached with the realization that the world he had helped reshape was now hurtling toward new challenges, a future where Rickey's guiding hand would be conspicuously absent. His profound belief that "a life is not important except in the impact it has on other lives" resonated even more deeply as he weighed the growing divide between preserving a cherished legacy and embracing the powerful forces of progress that threatened to diminish the very ideals he stood for, now under a new corporate helm focused on the bottom line. This did not mean there was animosity between him and O'Malley.

Walter O'Malley, Owner and Businessman

Meanwhile, having secured his position, Walter O'Malley pressed forward with his expansive vision, determined to propel baseball into the modern age. His bold installment strategies and innovative business maneuvers would not only redefine the economics of baseball but also set the stage for the sport's expansion into new markets and realms of media. He saw a future where baseball's appeal stretched far beyond its traditional urban strongholds, envisioning lucrative television deals and a broader national footprint. It was less about on-field scouting and more about market expansion and profitability. While Rickey, ever the baseball visionary, retreated to Pittsburgh hoping to fashion a new order, the foundational alterations he had wrought continued to underpin the game, profoundly imprinting on every prospect discovered and every barrier that was eventually shattered, a testament to his enduring influence even in absence.

The interplay of these monumental shifts—Rickey's passion for baseball's intrinsic development against O'Malley's pragmatism for its financial growth, of tradition against expansion—made the saga of baseball an ever-evolving dialogue. The boardroom deals and the echoes of cheering fans interwove the destinies of its architects: Rickey, whose ideals had ignited the flame of progress; O'Malley, whose ambition had fanned that flame into an inferno of modern enterprise, shaped by his relentless pursuit of a viable future for the franchise; and Robinson, whose contributions on and off the field had forever altered the fabric of American society, leaving an indelible mark on the nation's conscience.

As the Dodgers continued to evolve under O'Malley's sole leadership and the game's commercial heartbeat quickened with every televised match, one question lingered in the shadows of history: In the relentless pursuit of progress, did baseball sacrifice something irreplaceable in the boardroom battles that changed its leadership, particularly the human-centric approach that Rickey embodied? Or was the evolution itself the only way the game could survive the test of time, adapting to a changing America?

In the end, baseball's story endures as a constant balancing act between memory and innovation, a narrative where every stolen base, every whispered negotiation, and every visionary dream serves as a reminder that while the game's form may change, its enduring soul remains timeless. It is a testament to the complex forces that shape institutions. It is a poignant reflection on how personal ambition and economic realities intersect to redefine a cherished pastime, always moving forward yet forever looking back at its pivotal transformations.

Chapter Twelve
The Road to Relocation (1946-1955)

Brooklyn was more than a borough; it was a heartbeat, a defiant rhythm pounding through brownstone streets and trolley-lined avenues, a city within a city where baseball was gospel and Ebbets Field stood as its sacred temple. The faithful poured through its wrought-iron gates, a congregation in white and Dodger blue, waving scorecards like hymns, their voices rising in the immortal cadence of names that had long since become legends—Jackie Robinson, Duke Snider, Pee Wee Reese. Beneath those aging grandstands, fathers passed dreams to sons, the worn leather of their mitts carrying the weight of a thousand summers.

Nevertheless, time was a patient thief, stealing the years in whispers, eroding the edges of that old ballpark until its voice grew hoarse beneath the weight of progress. The wooden seats groaned against decades of devotion, the aisles too narrow for the crowds that still came, cheered, and clung to history. Brooklyn was changing, reshaping itself in the shadow of industry's retreat, as factories fell silent and families drifted toward the broad stretches of Long Island. The borough, once a stronghold of old-world pride, now teetered on the edge of reinvention, caught between past and future, between memory and necessity.

Walter O'Malley saw and experienced it all, from rust and crumbling cement to thinning crowds. He was not just a keeper of baseball but a steward of survival, and survival meant evolution. He turned to Emil Praeger, a master of steel and structure who had built floating fortresses during the war and envisioned stadiums that could defy the years. On October 14, 1946, Emil Praeger's letter arrived—a masterpiece not of prose but of vision. "They say everything happens in Brooklyn, but here is something that did not. Your fertile imagination should have some ideas about enlarging or replacing our present stadium." His pen would later carve a plan to reimagine the borough, placing the new stadium at the Atlantic and Flatbush Avenues confluence, where subway tunnels pulsed beneath the pavement like veins feeding the city. The Long Island Railroad terminal stood waiting like a gatekeeper for fans beyond the borough, a conduit that could carry the roar of Brooklyn to its outer limits. It is graphic proof that Walter O'Malley had already begun problem-solving in Brooklyn, not elsewhere. On October 22, 1946, Praeger responded to Walter O'Malley's letter about the possibility of replacing an aging Ebbets Field, stating, "I saw one of the last Brooklyn-St. Louis' games have followed this year's attendance record. Brooklyn could certainly use a larger stadium. You may be interested to know that at the request of Admiral Morell, I prepared a design for a proposed memorial stadium for Washington, D.C. I have some photographs of a model which was made of this design, renderings, and layout plans, and if you are interested in seeing them, I will be glad to have copies made and forwarded to you. Nothing quite like it has been built, and I think it has some exciting features. I have been out of the Navy for several months and have been busy on exciting projects."

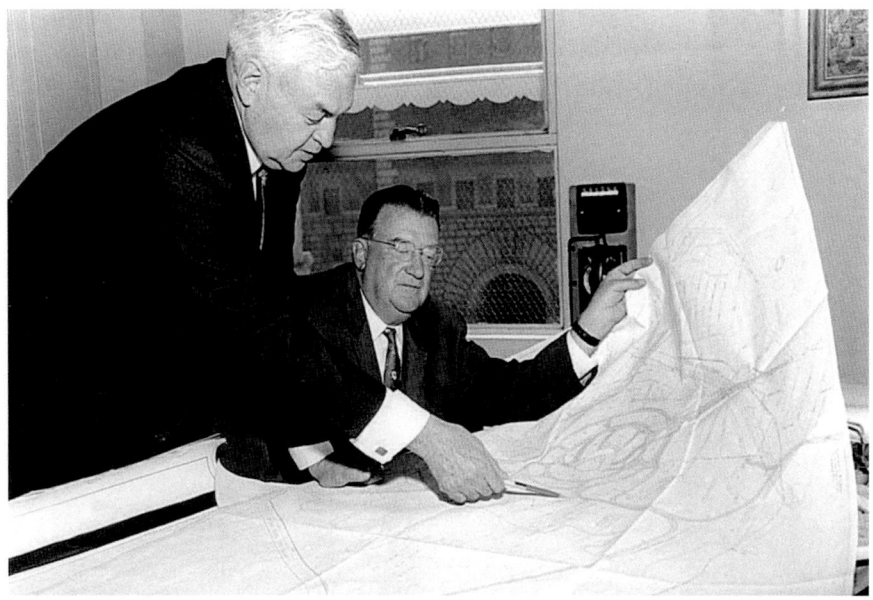

Emil Praeger spent the better part of the decade helping to keep the Dodgers in Brooklyn

It was no idle sketch—it was a blueprint for destiny. A ballpark rising from necessity and belief cemented in a place where Brooklyn still dreamed, fought, and stood resilient against the fading light of its golden age. Praeger, a naval engineer renowned for redefining structural durability, had built floating breakwaters during World War II, earning his reputation as one of the sharpest minds in civil engineering. If anyone could design the Brooklyn stadium of the future, it was him. His correspondence with O'Malley was precise, with bold ideas that would reshape Brooklyn baseball for generations. And yet, even as Brooklyn faded from the Dodgers' future, O'Malley was already laying the foundation for something new. Dodgertown, the team's Vero Beach, Florida, spring training facility, was another testament to his vision. In 1952, Emil Praeger submitted construction estimates for a 5,000-seat stadium in Vero Beach. Dodgertown was more than a training ground—it was a baseball sanctuary. In this place, the Dodgers could refine their craft, away from the political battles and bureaucratic entanglements of New York.

March 11, 1953, Walter O'Malley (left) and Bud Holman shake hands at Dedication Ceremonies for Holman Stadium, Dodgertown, Vero Beach, Florida. As an astute business and community leader, Holman saw and acted on the opportunity to bring the Dodgers and their many minor league teams to Vero Beach for spring training. The plaque presented by the Dodgers reads, "The Brooklyn Dodgers Dedicate Holman Stadium to Honor Bud L. Holman of the Friendly City of Vero Beach, Walter F. O'Malley, President, Emil H. Praeger, C.E., Designer, 1953."

On June 18, 1953, Walter O'Malley reached out to Robert Moses in a letter: "My problem is to get a ballpark one well located and with ample parking accommodations. This is a must if we are to keep our franchise in Brooklyn." It hardly sounds like someone set on moving to Los Angeles, and it is further evidence that Robert Moses was totally unaccommodating. Nonetheless, even the grandest visions must contend with the forces that guard the gates of change. Brooklyn had long been where innovation met resistance, and great ideas were entangled in bureaucracy. Walter O'Malley had the full backing of Governor Averell Harriman, who publicly voiced his support and signed Chapter 951 into law on April 21, 1956. Nearly a hundred politicians and sports figures gathered at Brooklyn Borough President John Cashmore's office to celebrate the occasion, believing it would set the foundation for the Dodgers' continued presence in Brooklyn.

Nevertheless, the stadium project was never just about baseball. It was about vision, infrastructure, and a city's identity. Moreover, it soon collided with the most significant political force in New York: Robert Moses. Moses was not a man who bent to sentimentality. To him, New York was a vast puzzle of highways, bridges, tunnels, and planned urban efficiency. He saw stadiums as pieces within a grand design, not as emotional landmarks to be preserved for nostalgia. He was not a baseball fan. Moses refused to budge. Brooklyn was not the future, he argued—Queens was. He envisioned the Dodgers playing in what would later become Shea Stadium, positioned strategically within his master plan. To Moses, it was all about traffic flow, regional accessibility, and logistics. Nevertheless, to O'Malley, it was about Brooklyn—the heartbeat of a city, the preservation of history.

April 21, 1956, (L-R) Dodger President Walter O'Malley; President, Borough of Brooklyn John Cashmore; Governor of New York Averell Harriman; and New York City Parks Commissioner Robert Moses. Harriman went to Brooklyn to sign a bill (Chapter 951 of the Laws of 1956) to establish the Brooklyn Sports Center Authority to improve the chances of a new baseball stadium in Brooklyn to replace aging Ebbets Field. Harriman vowed his support to O'Malley and the Dodgers.

"Queens Dodgers" sounds like an awkward mismatch of history and geography—like calling the Statue of Liberty "Jersey's Torch." The Dodgers were Brooklyn's soul, deeply woven into the borough's culture, neighborhoods, and people. Rebranding them as belonging to Queens would have betrayed everything they stood for. Brooklyn fans were fiercely loyal, not just to the team but to the borough itself. They did not cheer for the Dodgers simply because of the players—they cheered because the team was Brooklyn. The name "Brooklyn Dodgers" was not just a label; it was identity, courage, and heritage. It came from the days of trolley-dodging pedestrians, a symbol of working-class resilience. Uprooting them to

Queens would have felt like stripping them of their essence, forcing them into a name that had no emotional resonance. Queens was not Brooklyn. It did not have the same entrenched baseball history. It was not Ebbets Field. It was not the heart of a borough that bled Dodger blue. O'Malley knew this—he understood that a move to Queens would alienate the fans who had sustained the team for generations. That is why he fought for Brooklyn and envisioned a new stadium within its borders rather than accepting Robert Moses' push to relocate them to Queens. Had the team become the "Queens Dodgers," it likely would not have survived in New York. The fanbase would have fractured, leaving the team stranded in a borough that never felt like home. Brooklyn would have mourned the loss just the same because once they left Ebbets Field, the team's heart went with them. In short, "Queens Dodgers" was never going to work. Brooklyn Dodgers? That was destiny. Queens Dodgers? That was a bureaucratic afterthought with no soul. O'Malley saw it, the fans knew it, and history proved that Brooklyn's baseball fate lay elsewhere.

Even as O'Malley pressed forward, political delays mounted. The Brooklyn Sports Center Authority, formed to oversee stadium construction, became ensnared in legislative bottlenecks, unable to cut through the red tape needed to secure land. Time was slipping away, and O'Malley knew it. Frustration turned to ink, O'Malley's hand steady as he wrote his vision into history, a plea not for funding but for freedom—to build, dream, and carve a future where baseball could last. In a letter to William Tracy, Vice Chairman of the Triborough Bridge and Tunnel Authority, O'Malley spelled it out: "I believe a new ballpark should be built, financed, and owned by the ball club. It should occupy land on the tax roll. The only assistance I am looking for is assembling a suitable plot, and I hope the mechanics of Title I (of the 1949 Housing Act) could be used if the ballpark were also used as a parking garage." It was not a desperate plea—this was clarity. O'Malley was not asking for government funding or handouts. He was asking for the right to build, to create something that would last. Nevertheless, the forces aligned against him showed no signs of compromise.

Even as Brooklyn fought its bureaucratic battle, another team—the New York Giants — found itself at a crossroads. Horace Stoneham had initially planned to relocate his franchise to Minneapolis, where he would disband his Triple-A affiliate and start fresh. Nevertheless, O'Malley saw things differently. He understood that baseball's future was not merely about moving teams—it was about sustaining rivalries, maintaining competitive balance, and ensuring the survival of the National League's identity. Air travel had erased the logistical barriers of cross-country scheduling, making West Coast expansion more viable than ever. So, O'Malley convinced Stoneham to abandon Minneapolis and join him on an entirely new frontier: San Francisco. All this was finally decided during a hunting trip to Wyoming.

Brooklyn's loss of the Dodgers was not just a sports story; it mirrored the tectonic shifts across postwar America. The 1940s and '50s were a time of rapid urban transformation, with suburban expansion, highway construction, and changing economic centers altering the fabric of many cities. Dwight D. Eisenhower's Interstate Highway System was one of American history's most transformative infrastructure projects. The Federal-Aid Highway Act, signed into law on June 29, 1956, created a vast network of controlled-access highways designed for efficiency, defense, and economic growth. However, this also added to potential future turmoil. Once a powerhouse of industry, Brooklyn witnessed the retreat of manufacturing and the rise of suburban migration as families moved to Long Island and beyond. The potential relocation of the Dodgers was emblematic of this future transition; what once made Brooklyn vibrant and self-sustaining was now giving way to a more dispersed metropolitan existence. Infrastructure projects like Robert Moses' massive highway expansions fundamentally reshaped communities. The preference for automobiles over public transit reflected a new vision of urban planning, prioritizing accessibility to growing suburban areas rather than reinforcing the density of traditional city centers. In many ways, O'Malley's battle was not just about baseball; it was about the fight between an old, neighborhood-centric urban model and the sprawling, automobile-driven future Moses championed.

However, even as Brooklyn faded from the Dodgers' future, O'Malley laid the foundation for something new. Dodgertown, the team's Vero Beach, Florida, spring training facility, was another testament to his vision. In 1952, Emil Praeger, the same engineer who had dreamed up Brooklyn's future stadium, submitted construction estimates for a 5,000-seat stadium in Vero Beach. Dodgertown was more than a training ground—it was a baseball sanctuary. In this place, the Dodgers could refine their craft, away from the political battles and bureaucratic entanglements of New York. The fight for Brooklyn's baseball soul was slipping into its final innings, the clock ticking toward a future neither borough nor ballpark could outrun. The Dodgers still played beneath the aging beams of Ebbets Field, but its foundation trembled—not from the weight of history, but from the forces aligning beyond its gates.

Walter O'Malley had spent years pushing against immovable obstacles, the ink of his letters drying before they could bend New York's bureaucratic machine. Politicians' promises were fading echoes, drowned out by Robert Moses's rigid resolve, whose vision of urban efficiency saw no place for sentiment or baseball. The great chess match between them had stretched for a decade, but now the pieces were nearing their final moves. Even within the Dodgers' clubhouse, whispers were growing. The players could feel the uncertainty, the tension, the quiet realization that the future would not wait for Brooklyn to catch up. O'Malley was not merely chasing a stadium anymore; he was chasing survival, carving out a path where baseball could endure beyond the crumbling facades of Ebbets Field. However, despite the looming inevitability, Brooklyn's "faithful" still filled the stands, cheered, and clung to the hope that history was too sacred to be rewritten. They waved their scorecards like prayer books, their voices rising into the night air, unaware that they were witnesses to the final summer of Brooklyn baseball as they knew it. For now, the Dodgers were still there. Nevertheless, the cracks beneath them grew and soon became a chasm.

BROOKLYN DODGERS AT EBBETS FIELD 1913-1957

Walter O'Malley meets with New York City officials regarding a new ballpark in Brooklyn for the Dodgers on Aug. 19, 1955. The meeting at Gracie Mansion included New York Mayor Robert Wagner (far left), Robert Moses, Parks Commissioner for the City of New York and Brooklyn Borough President John Cashmore (far right)

Chapter Thirteen
The Dodgers' Golden Age (1949-1956)

Brooklyn's soul was forged at Ebbets Field—a venerable sanctuary whose weathered brick walls reverberated with the roar of passionate fans, while the tantalizing tang of sizzling hot dogs mingled with the aroma of freshly cut grass. Over these transformative years, the Brooklyn Dodgers transcended mere sport. They evolved from scrappy warriors into living legends; every swing of the bat, every strike of a pitch, every stolen base, and every breathtaking catch inscribed dreams deep into the collective heart of a borough that cherished athletic artistry and celebrated its heroic icons. This golden era was marked by breakthrough rookie debuts, marquee awards, record-shattering performances, and moments of sublime brilliance—each one a note in a symphony of hope, sacrifice, and glory that continues to echo through the annals of baseball.

1949: A Series of Daring Moments and Heart-Stopping Drama

In the storied year of 1949, the Brooklyn Dodgers carved an indelible mark into baseball's lore—a season as dramatic and sweeping as a grand operatic performance on the emerald stage. The team charged through the National League, boasting a formidable 97-57 record, an achievement that radiated with both gritty determination and poetic brilliance.

At the heart of this epoch was Jackie Robinson, who transformed every at-bat into an act of daring artistry. Robinson's bat danced through the season with a batting average of .342, and his fleet-footed dash stole 37 bases, making each stolen base a fleeting stroke of genius that earned him the National League MVP. His performance was a vivid tapestry of athletic grace and audacity—a symbol of passion and progress that both inspired and dazzled the nation.

*1949 Rookie of the year and his favorite "target" catcher Roy Campanella
photo from author's Dodger Museum Collection*

On the pitching mound, rookie phenom Don Newcombe emerged like a tempest in full bloom. With a season tally of 17 wins, a 3.17 ERA, and 149 strikeouts, he etched his name in the annals of history as the NL Rookie of the Year. Newcombe's prowess culminated in an unforgettable Game 1 of the World Series, where he hurled a complete game and struck out 11 Yankee batters—a display of formidable skill and raw power. Yet even his valiant performance was met with the cruel poetry of baseball when a late, dramatic walk-off home run by Tommy Henrich denied him a win in a 1-0 defeat.

Preacher Roe the "Wizard from the Ozarks" from author's Dodger Museum Collection

The World Series itself was a stage of epic contrasts—a series where brilliance intermingled with heartbreak. In Game 2, the resolute arm of

Preacher Roe delivered a sublime six-hit shutout, a masterclass in pitching that momentarily lifted the Dodgers from despair. Bolstered by timely heroics from Jackie Robinson, whose sharp double ignited a fleeting surge of hope, the team displayed flashes of their innate brilliance. Nonetheless, the relentless power of the New York Yankees prevailed, clinching the series 4-1 and painting the final chapter with hues both triumphant for the victors and tragically bittersweet for Brooklyn.

This 1949 odyssey of soaring highs and gut-wrenching lows remains one of baseball's most evocative narratives—a season lit by the fire of innovation, courage, and artistry that continues to resonate across the ages

1950: The Tragic Loss to the Phillies

In the tapestry of baseball history, few seasons shimmer with as many poignant contrasts as 1950—a year when the Brooklyn Dodgers dazzled with a collective brilliance yet found themselves undone by fate on a chilly October day. On October 1, 1950, as autumn's golden light softened the edges of Ebbets Field and every crack of the bat carried the weight of dreams, the Dodgers charged down the field with a season defined by unity and raw offensive power. That year, the team's ferocious lineup ignited a staggering 847 runs, the highest in the National League tribute to their cohesive and artful attack even as no single Dodger claimed a major individual statistical crown. Icons like Jackie Robinson, with his resolute average of .328, Gil Hodges, Duke Snider, and Roy Campanella poured their hearts into every play, their contributions weaving together the poetic ambition of a team that shone as brightly as any individual star, even if none stood alone at the pinnacle of league statistics.

"Blue Bombers" dominated Golden age era: first row Jackie Robinson, Carl Furillo, Pee Wee Reese second row Roy Campanella, Gil Hodges, Duke Snider Colorized photo by Author

As the season's final act unfolded in the tenth inning of that decisive contest, the stage at Ebbets Field became a theater of destiny. With the score locked in a tense deadlock, the atmosphere heavy with anticipation, Dick Sisler stepped to the plate like a seasoned protagonist in a grand drama. In one sublime, gravity-defying swing, his bat unleashed a home run that carved an incandescent arc across the crisp October sky—a moment that sealed the game and ensured the National League pennant slipped into the hands of the Philadelphia Phillies' youthful "Whiz Kids." That hit, breathtaking and bittersweet in its finality, transformed the very air into a canvas emblazoned with both the agony of defeat and the enduring poetry of hope.

Thus, the 1950 season stands as both a tribute to the indomitable spirit of the Dodgers and a reminder that even in the absence of individual accolades, the power of collective artistry on the diamond can create legends.

1951: The Dark Turn and the Admission of Cheating

In the luminous yet turbulent summer of 1951, the Brooklyn Dodgers embarked on a season both brilliant and bittersweet—a campaign illuminated by the radiant hopes of postseason glory yet marred by shadows that would haunt a hero for decades to come. In an era when the glare of television cameras met the raw intensity of live ballgames, every mound appearance was a statement of ambition and courage. At the heart of this unfolding drama was Ralph Branca, once celebrated as the shining promise of Brooklyn's pitching staff. His deliveries, once a master class in artistry and control, carried with them the weight of Brooklyn's collective dreams.

Then came that fateful postseason game—a moment suspended in time. Under the piercing lights and before a nation tethered to every pitch, Branca unleashed one performance that was both exquisite and devastating. In that heightened instant, his every motion bespoke the poetry of the game until an ill-timed pitch, destined to be forever intertwined with heartbreak, soared into baseball lore. In the ensuing dust and roar, opposing batter Bobby Thomson's monumental home run became the arrow that pierced the Dodgers' hopes—a swing that not only sealed the fate of the contest but also marked the beginning of a transformation in Branca's career.

BROOKLYN DODGERS AT EBBETS FIELD 1913-1957

Walter O'Malley, Chuck Dressen, Ralph Branca and his wife Ann Mulvey

Decades later, long after the cheers had dwindled into echoes of memory, a damning revelation surfaced. With a daunting 13½-game deficit looming by August, the New York Giants had engineered an ingenious and sinister sign-stealing system. Discreet buzzers and clandestine mechanical cues, carefully relayed from their center-field clubhouse, had provided the Giants with an unfair advantage. This admission of deception cast a long, somber shadow over that fateful pitch, suggesting that even the purest display of talent—Branca's once dazzling artistry—could be irrevocably tainted by underhanded tactics. The revelation turned the home run into not just a moment of personal failure but a symbol of an era rife with both brilliance and betrayal.

In the immediate aftermath, despite Branca's respectable 13–12 record and a 3.26 ERA for the season, that singular pitch became a turning point from which his brilliance could never fully recover. The physical toll of countless high-pressure outings, combined with the relentless burden of that defining moment, eroded the velocity and precision that had once captivated baseball fans. His subsequent performances, whether with subsequent stints with the Dodgers or brief forays with other teams, never managed to recapture the incandescent magic of those early years. Yet, in the twilight of his career, off the field, Branca found a measure of redemption as he devoted himself to the baseball community—offering guidance and preserving the dignity that had been so imperiled on that unforgettable day.

Thus, the 1951 season remains etched as an epic of soaring hopes and crushing setbacks—a narrative where the brilliance of Brooklyn's collective play was punctuated by a single, cheating, sorrowful act that reshaped a career and altered the course of baseball history

1952: A Symphony of Record, Redemption, and No-Hitters

In 1952, the Brooklyn Dodgers emerged as a singular force on the diamond, finishing the regular season with an enviable record of 96 57—a

1952 Topps Ralph Branca card from author's Dodger Museum Collection

stately reflection of their determination and collective brilliance. That year, the Dodgers orchestrated an offensive masterpiece, leading the National League in runs scored, home runs, and stolen bases—a tapestry of plays woven by every member of the club.

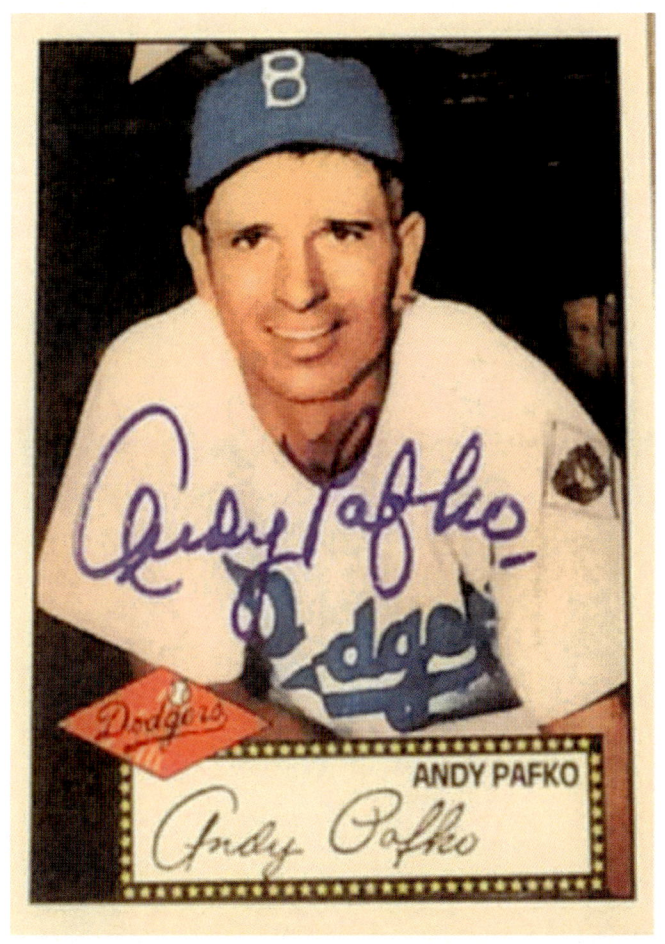

1952 Andy Pafko Topps card # 1 (impossible to find in mint Condition) from authors Dodgers Museum Collection

At the heart of that vibrant offensive display was Gil Hodges, whose contributions added a layer of unstoppable power to the team's lineup. Anchoring the Dodgers at first base, Hodges led the team with a majestic 32 home runs, 27 doubles, 102 RBI, and 107 walks, finishing with a .500 slugging percentage. His performance wasn't merely a string of numbers but a display of raw, untamed grit and a testament to his profound impact on the game. His towering swings, timely drives, and sure-handed play helped propel the Dodgers' potent offense, complementing the finesse of teammates like Jackie Robinson and the audacious base-stealing flair of Pee Wee Reese.

1950 Northland Bread end label (impossible to find) from author's Dodger Museum Collection

The narrative of that season crescendoed under the bright lights of post-season baseball. Switching from the rugged regular-season battlegrounds to the exalted stage of the World Series, the Dodgers faced the perennial juggernaut, the New York Yankees, in an epic seven-game duel. Under the sparkling autumn skies at Ebbets Field and Yankee Stadium, every pitch and every hit glowed with the promise of glory. While the series was punctuated by stellar moments—from Duke Snider's heroic home runs to the gritty resolve of Brooklyn's entire roster—the clamor of victory ultimately belonged to the Yankees, who clinched the series in a nail-biting Game 7.

1952 Star Cal Decal of Gil Hodges and Pee Wee Resse from Authors Dodger Museum Collection

Yet even in the bittersweet loss, the legacy of 1952 endures. The season's record of 96 57, the collective offensive dominance, and the sterling contributions of Gil Hodges weave together a story of passion, perseverance, and teamwork. It stands as a reminder that, in the grand narrative of baseball, the magic lies as much in the symphony of a team effort as in the singular brilliance of its individual stars.

1953: A Year of Aerial Miracles, Explosive Determination, and Record-Setting Moments

In 1953, the Brooklyn Dodgers soared to an almost mythic plateau, finishing the regular season with a record of 105 49—the highest winning percentage in franchise history at approximately .682. This season was a masterclass in collective excellence, where every inning shimmered with talent, determination, and narrative-defining moments.

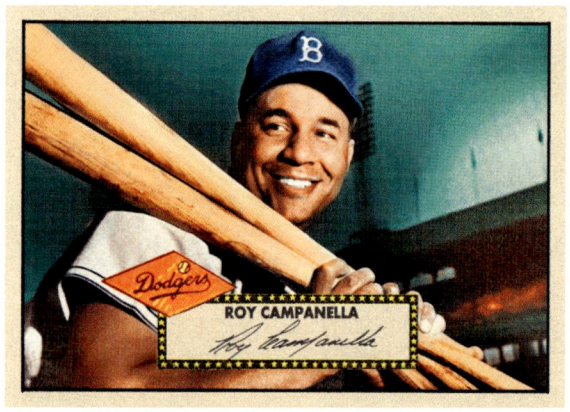

1952 Topps Alternate Artwork from Author's Dodger Museum Collection

BROOKLYN DODGERS AT EBBETS FIELD 1913-1957

1953 Brooklyn Dodgers 105-59 .689 winning percentage is highest in team history. Photo from author's Dodger Museum Collection.

At the heart of this luminous campaign, Roy Campanella commanded the plate with poise and power—earning his second National League MVP award while smashing 41 home runs batting in 142 runs with a .312 average—while rookie Jim Gilliam burst onto the scene to claim the NL Rookie of the Year honor, infusing the team with fresh promise. On the offensive front, Duke Snider led the National League with an awe-inspiring 42 home runs, each one a defiant declaration of his power, and Carl Furillo quietly dazzled by capturing the league's batting title with a .344 average. Meanwhile, Pee Wee Reese lent his speed to the team's dynamic by leading the club with 22 stolen bases, ensuring that every run was chased down with relentless energy.

1953 Bowman Color card # 78 of Carl Furillo from author's Dodger Museum Collection

In the heat of postseason drama, the World Series against the perennial juggernaut, spurred by Jake Ruperts beer money, the New York Yankees, transformed the season into an epic saga. Carl Erskine delivered a masterful performance in Game 3 with a record-setting 14 strikeouts, his pitches falling like precise brushstrokes on a timeless canvas. Roy Campanella then ignited hope with a decisive, tie breaking home run that reverberated through Ebbets Field. Duke Snider contributed with clutch doubles and a timely home run in Game 4, his bat carving a path of resistance against the overwhelming Yankees force.

Duke Snider roams Outfield of Ebbets Field from Author's Dodger Museum Collection.

1953 Bowman Color Carl Erskine card # 12 From author's Dodger Museum Collection

Amid these high-voltage moments, Jackie Robinson, the trailblazer whose name had become synonymous with courage and brilliance—stepped forward with a blend of athletic virtuosity and unwavering determination. In the World Series, Robinson's performance transcended mere statistics. With his defiant gaze and fearless baserunning, he not only punctuated critical moments with daring steals but orchestrated key defensive saves that shifted momentum in the Dodgers' favor. One can recall the electric atmosphere when Robinson, barreling down the line, executed a daring steal that not only put him in scoring position but also embodied the spirit of a team that played with both grace and grit. His agile defensive plays—marked by acrobatic catches and swift throws—were as much a part of the narrative as his leadership on the field, inspiring his teammates and resonating deeply with every fan in the stands.

1953 National League MVP Roy Campanella from author's Dodger Museum Collection.

Yet, even as these stellar individual performances lit up the postseason stage, the ultimate prize eluded the Dodgers. The Yankees triumphed in the series, 4 2, a bittersweet end to a season defined by both record-setting brilliance and moments of heart-stopping near-miss glory. The legacy of the 1953 Brooklyn Dodgers lives on—a tapestry interwoven with shining individual achievements like Campanella's MVP heroics, Snider's towering swings, Furillo's smooth precision at the plate, Reese's fleet-footed daring, and Robinson's transcendent blend of skill and resolve.

ALLEN SCHERY

1954: A Year of Shattered Dreams and Soul-Stirring Loss

In 1954, under the steady guidance of manager Walter Alston, the Brooklyn Dodgers compiled a strong 92 62 record—even though they finished second in the National League, their season was marked by a consistency that spoke to the strength of every link in the chain.

While the 1954 campaign didn't yield the marquee individual league-leading honors of the previous year, several Dodger stars remained among the league's elite. Jackie Robinson continued to dazzle with his combination of refined hitting, brilliant defense, and blazing speed. His tireless running and smart baserunning kept him near the top of the stolen base rankings—a hallmark of his game that consistently troubled opposing defenses.

Similarly, Duke Snider maintained his reputation as a formidable power hitter. Though his home run totals dipped slightly from his record-setting 1953 performance, Snider's slugging still placed him among the league's notable run producers, slamming 40 home runs, knocking in 130 runs while hitting a career high .341. Alongside him, Carl Furillo continued to post a polished batting average, demonstrating an unwavering consistency at the plate. Together, they formed a potent offensive unit that drove the Dodgers to score 778 runs over the season—a reflection of a lineup that, even without several outright league crowns, proved to be one of the most balanced and dangerous in the NL.

BROOKLYN DODGERS AT EBBETS FIELD 1913-1957

In 1954 The New York Journal Newspaper issued the reward coupons. Here is the complete set collected by the author from back then 71 years ago.

On the mound, Brooklyn's pitching staff—anchored by the ever-reliable Preacher Roe and complemented by Don Newcombe—turned in workmanlike and clutch performances throughout the season. While none of the Dodgers' pitchers dominated the league statistics in a headline-grabbing way in 1954, their collective efforts often kept the games close. Their ability to limit opponents to 740 runs over the season underscored a rotation that, though it may have lacked a singular transcendent ace, was nevertheless a critical component of the team's success.

Thus, although 1954 did not produce a slew of individual league-leading statistical honors for the Dodgers, the season was imbued with a quiet brilliance. The contributions from Robinson, Snider, Furillo, and the pitching staff ensured that every game was played with passion and precision. Their combined efforts laid the groundwork for future triumphs while reinforcing the legacy of Brooklyn baseball as a museum of consistent, collective excellence.

1955: The Triumph of a Forged Brotherhood—and a Home Run Barrage Amid an MVP Snub

The 1955 Brooklyn Dodgers season was a mythic odyssey a dazzling pageant of explosive beginnings, transcendent individual feats, and collective valor that forever redefined the soul of Brooklyn baseball. The campaign burst into life with an astonishing 11-game winning streak that set Ebbets Field ablaze with hope and promise. From that glowing start, the Dodgers mounted a season of staggering achievement. Duke Snider emerged as a veritable colossus at the plate, smashing 42 home runs that soared like brilliant comets across the firmament, while his fleet-footed dashes injected each inning with a kinetic, almost balletic dynamism. Jackie Robinson, the indefatigable trailblazer, roamed the diamond with breathtaking audacity—his legendary steal of home epitomizing the rebellious, unyielding spirit of Brooklyn. Guiding the team with regal authority, Roy Campanella dominated behind the plate, orchestrating the play with majestic precision and earning his third National League MVP award, even as fervid debates swirled over whether Snider's incandescent offensive fireworks might have more rightly captured the honor. Complementary heroes in this epic included Gil Hodges and Sandy Amoros, whose timely, picture-perfect plays lent an indelible luster to an offensive symphony that consistently led the league in scoring and stolen bases.

On the mound, the Dodgers' pitching staff was a canvas painted with both venerable mastery and emerging brilliance. Don Newcombe's artful control and unyielding precision set a high standard from the very beginning, while the luminous Johnny Podres—who, on his 23rd birthday, delivered an awe-inspiring performance that rekindled Brooklyn's long-quenched hopes—became the season's destined champion. In critical junctures, rookie Roger Craig stepped forward, offering six-plus innings of resolute, poetic pitching that stymied the Yankees' relentless firepower. Meanwhile, the subtle debut of Sandy Koufax hinted at a forthcoming revolution in Dodgers pitching, whispering promises of transformative brilliance that would one day enshrine him among the very immortals of the game.

1956 Topps Don Newcombe #235 from Author's Dodger Museum Collection.

The apotheosis of this incandescent journey unfurled in the 1955 World Series—a seven-game epic against the indomitable New York Yankees that wove together heart-pounding tension, soul-stirring heroics, and ultimate redemption. At Yankee Stadium in Game 1, under the harsh glare of unyielding floodlights, Brooklyn's dreams were nearly dashed in a 6 5 loss—a contest punctuated by Jackie Robinson's audacious steal of home, a single moment of defiant brilliance that encapsulated the team's indomitable spirit.

Game One 1955 World Series Jackie Robinson steals home colorized by author and in his Dodger Museum Collection.

In Game 2, the Yankees, led by veteran left-hander Tommy Byrne, showcased their seasoned mastery to secure a 4 2 victory, deepening the narrative's tension and setting an arduous challenge for the Brooklyn faithful.

The winds of fate took a dramatic turn in Game 3 when the battleground returned to the cherished turf of Ebbets Field; that illuminated evening, on his birthday, Johnny Podres delivered a near-mythical performance, taming the Yankees to a mere three runs while igniting an emphatic 8 3 triumph that reawakened hope across Brooklyn.

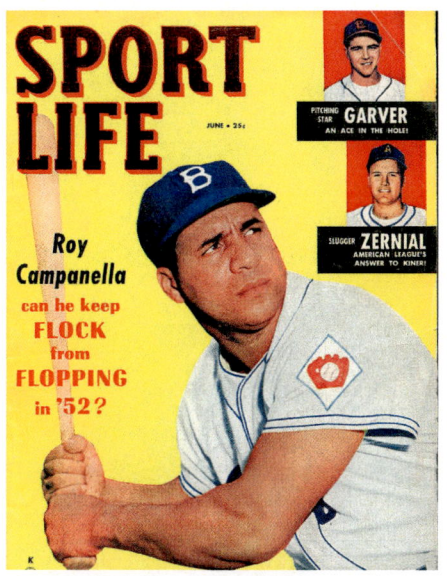

Sport Life June 1952 from Author's Dodger Museum Collection.

As twilight draped Ebbets Field in an almost surreal glow in Game 4, Roy Campanella's decisive, tie breaking home run rang out like a clarion call, while Duke Snider and Gil Hodges layered the offense with clutch extra-base hits, culminating in an 8 5 victory that evened the series and deepened the burgeoning sense of redemption. Game 5 found rookie Roger Craig once again summoning sublime precision on the mound; with over six innings of artful, resolute pitching complemented by Jackie Robinson's daring acrobatics on the bases, Brooklyn secured a critical 5 3 win to claim their first series lead. Yet the Yankees, ever tenacious, rallied in Game 6 with a commanding 5 1 triumph that set the stage for a final, epochal confrontation.

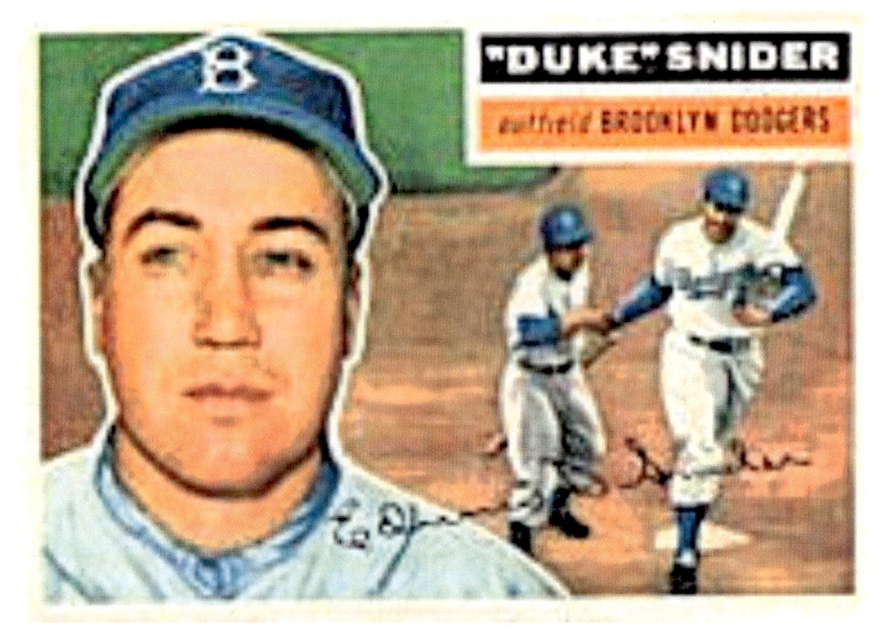

1956 Topps Duke Snider #156 from Author's Dodger Museum Collection.

Under the incandescent spotlight of Game 7 at Yankee Stadium, destiny unfurled its grand finale. With an entire city's pulse suspended in the hush between pitches, the drama on the field reached its zenith. In the midst of this high-stakes battle, a singular act of defensive brilliance vaulted into legend: in the bottom of the sixth inning, as a deep fly ball threatened to spark a Yankees rally, Sandy Amoros—recently introduced into the fray from the bench—sprang into action. With an almost preternatural burst of speed and graceful determination, Amoros surged from left field, extended his glove as if guided by fate, and made a breathtaking one-handed catch that defied both gravity and expectation. In a seamless display of athletic finesse, he immediately released the ball on a razor-quick throw to the infield, initiating a double play that stifled New York's momentum and preserved a precious lead. That singular moment, a fusion of instinct and artistry, would echo throughout the remainder of the game as a turning point that underscored the Dodgers' unyielding resolve.

Sandy Amoros series saving catch in game seven of 55 classic. Photo from Author's Dodger Museum Collection.

With the stage thus set, Johnny Podres returned to the mound to compose a complete-game masterpiece—a methodical, poetic dismantling of the Yankees' formidable lineup that culminated in an emphatic 2 0 triumph. Each pitch was a stroke of genius, every stride a testament to the years of bitter near-misses transformed, at long last, into a transcendent moment of jubilant victory. Crowned as the World Series MVP, Podres' heroic performance sealed Brooklyn's long-coveted championship, ending decades of heartbreak and enshrining the team in sporting immortality.

ALLEN SCHERY

To the victor goes the spoils as Series MVP Johnny Podres receives 1955 Corvette from Sport Magazine. Photo from the author's Dodger Museum Collection. Picture found at a Sports Collectors Convention in Brooklyn 50 years ago.

Thus, the 1955 season remains an epic chronicle of incandescent beginnings and resplendent heroics—a luminous tapestry woven from explosive stolen bases, thunderous home runs, and masterful pitching marvels. It is a saga replete with passionate controversies, timeless legends, and the foretold debut of future champions—a seamless symphony of passion and perseverance that forever enshrines the Brooklyn Dodgers in the annals of baseball lore. Long after the final echoes faded, Brooklyn's heartbeat remained—a rhythm kept alive in the stories, the legends, and the unwavering love of those who once called Ebbets Field home.

1956: The Final Ode to Ebbets Field and a Lasting No-Hitter Legacy

Then came 1956—a season destined to be forever emblazoned in memory as Brooklyn prepared for its final World Series game on home soil. On that tempestuous, rain-soaked night, Ebbets Field itself appeared to weep; the cool, damp air carried the scent of wet concrete intermingled with the nostalgic aroma of freshly popped popcorn, while the stadium's brilliant lights—once steadfast beacons of hope and raucous celebration—gradually softened into a reflective twilight beneath an overcast, sorrowful sky. In this charged atmosphere of farewell, Sal Maglie emerged as a pitching tempest, his fastballs and curveballs hurled with the raw, unyielding power of nature itself. Every pitch he delivered carried a final, resolute message—a defiant last stand against the inexorable march of time.

Sal "the Barber" Maglie pitched a no-hitter for Dodgers in 1956 above 1957 Topps card # 5 From Author's Dodger Museum Collection.

That season also celebrated the timeless mastery of the Dodgers' pitching staff through feats so flawless they bordered on legend. Alongside Carl Erskine's celebrated masterpieces, Sal Maglie etched his own legacy with a transcendent 5–0 no-hit performance—a moment that resonated as the final heartbeat of perfection before the curtain fell on a golden age. Every stolen base evoked the pioneering dash of Jackie Robinson; every gravity-defying catch honored the heroic leap of Sandy Amoros; and every powerful swing conjured the iconic blasts of Duke Snider. In the labyrinth of numbers that defined baseball's epic narrative, the 1956 Dodgers illuminated the stat sheets with a record of 93 wins and 61 losses, seizing the National League crown as if affirming that greatness endures beyond any farewell. Within that brilliant banner of success, individual splendor shone: Don Newcombe dominated the mound with such virtuosity that he not only steered the team to its lofty record but also captured both the National League MVP and the inaugural Cy Young Award—a dual honor that testified to his unassailable command on the pitch. Meanwhile, Duke Snider's 43 towering home runs lit up the scoreboards like blazing comets, each a sparkling tribute to the indomitable spirit of Brooklyn. These statistics—etched in the ledger of a legendary season—transcended mere numbers, transforming into an enduring symbol of triumph amid the bittersweet cadence of farewell. As the final out was recorded and the floodlights gradually surrendered to a profound, almost sacred silence, Brooklyn was enveloped in a reflective stillness—a living elegy that immortalized an era defined by both magnificent triumph and tender goodbye.

Yet, as the regular season closed with Sal Maglie's mystical no-hit masterpiece still echoing in the hearts of the faithful, destiny beckoned for one final, epic chapter: the 1956 World Series.

Sal Maglie PM-10 Stadium Pin worn on Author's Tee Shirt 1956-1957

Across a seven-game odyssey, each contest became a verse in a ballad of passion and perseverance. On October 3 at Ebbets Field, the Dodgers opened their postseason campaign with a rousing 6–3 triumph. Under a sky heavy with both promise and portent, Duke Snider ignited the offense with a towering, breathtaking home run that split the stormy heavens; Roy Campanella, the stalwart behind the plate, orchestrated the defensive symphony with unwavering calm; and Pee Wee Reese's fleet footed dashes set the pace, repelling the Yankee charge with every graceful movement. Barely had the echoes of that opening victory begun to subside when, on October 5, Brooklyn unleashed an offensive maelstrom, outscoring the Yankees 13–8 in an electrifying display where every hit was a defiant spark against the gathering gloom—Snider's bat carving deep arcs through the rain, extra-base bursts from Gil Hodges and Carl Furillo fueling the rally, while Jackie Robinson's daring base running electrified the infield.

The drama then swept to Yankee Stadium for Game 3 on October 6, where, amid the storied confines of New York's revered fortress, the Dodgers battled valiantly in a 5–3 loss. Even in defeat, the determined spirit of Brooklyn shone through: timely hits by Snider and the ceaseless hustles of Reese and Robinson punctuated the contest as the Yankees' measured rally nudged them ahead. The following night, on October 7, Brooklyn fought with every fiber of its being as the Yankees clinched a 6–2 victory; yet every determined swing and graceful defensive play—from Campanella's masterful guidance to Hodges' dependable ground balls—spoke to a resilience that defied the bitter taste of defeat. Then, on October 8, the world paused in hushed awe at Yankee Stadium as Don Larsen ascended to legendary status with his flawless perfect game—a 2–0 masterpiece, where every pitch was a stroke of genius, and even Brooklyn's silence resonated with both admiration and regret.

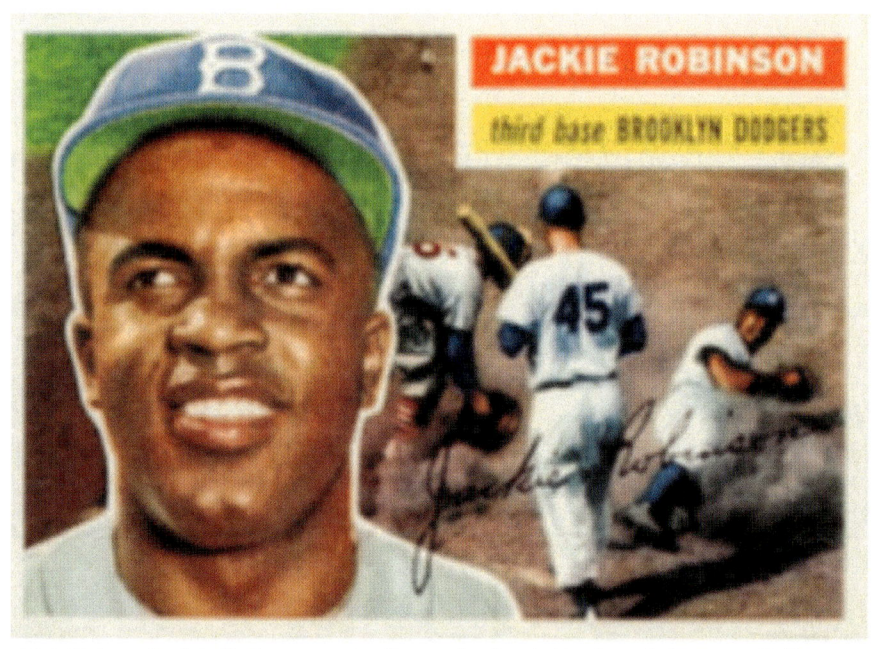

1956 Topps Jackie Robinson #39 from Author's Dodger Museum Collection.

Returning to their cherished home on October 9, the Dodgers engineered one of the series' most dramatic moments in a grueling extra-inning duel. In a single, hard-fought contest that stretched over 10 nail-biting innings, every pitch and every heartbeat at Ebbets Field carried the weight of hope and legacy. With meticulous precision and the collective grit of an entire borough, Brooklyn secured a razor-thin 1–0 victory—a triumph decisively achieved by the astonishing performance of reliever Labine. Though typically summoned for fleeting moments, Labine rose to the occasion in the twilight hours, masterfully quieting the Yankees' assault and etching his name in that pivotal game. Stellar defensive plays—from Jackie Robinson's acrobatic stops to Gil Hodges' unwavering ground balls—complemented a timely, solitary run that broke the deadlock, underscoring Brooklyn's indomitable will.

1956 Topps Clem Labine #180 from Author's Dodger Museum Collection.

In the grand finale on October 10 at Ebbets Field, fate delivered a crushing 9–0 demolition as the Yankees, imbued with the fervor of redemption and destiny fulfilled, closed the series with resounding victory. Even amid overwhelming adversity, Brooklyn's heroes—Snider with his steadfast, determined swings, Robinson with his relentless, electrifying dashes along the baselines, and Campanella with his unwavering command behind the plate—fought with valor, ensuring that every heroic gesture and every fleeting moment of grace would be remembered, even in heartbreak.

Thus, from the season's passionate closing moments—embodied by Sal Maglie's transcendent no-hit performance—and the rain-slicked, incandescent battles of the World Series, the saga of 1956 unfolds as a vibrant mosaic. Every game is a vivid chapter, every play a resonant verse in the eternal hymn of Brooklyn's immortal legacy. It is a ballad of triumph and sorrow, of bold swings and quiet heroism, indelibly etched into the heart of America's favorite pastime—a legacy that, even as time marches inexorably on, refuses to be forgotten. Brooklyn fans did not realize it but the muses would never let them see another World Series game.

Epilogue: A Legacy Etched in Time

From the daring sparks of 1949—set against nights resounding with roaring cheers and the resolute clatter of uniforms—to the soul-shattering collapse against the Phillies in 1950; from the dark revelations and bitter lessons of 1951 to the record-shattering brilliance of no-hitter perfection and the quirky genius showcased in 1952 and 1953; through the heart-wrenching sorrow of 1954 and the triumphant redemption of 1955—where Duke Snider's luminous home run crown ignited the heavens even as his hard-fought MVP dreams went unmet, and Roy Campanella's triple mantle of MVP awards underscored a legacy of unwavering leadership—and finally, to the tear-stained farewell of 1956, marked by everlasting no-hit legacies and the poignant final notes of a storied chapter—the Dodgers' Golden Age remains an indelible tapestry of passion, perseverance, and poetic beauty.

Every stolen base, every strikeout, every breathtaking catch, and every majestic home run forms a timeless note in the everlasting symphony of Brooklyn. Though Ebbets Field now exists only as a cherished, faded beacon on the horizon of memory, its indefatigable spirit endures as a luminous light—a cosmic guide for every dreamer, every ball player, and every soul who dares to believe that in the face of adversity, true greatness is forever within reach.

Chapter Fourteen
It Comes Undone (1956-1957)

Brooklyn was more than a borough; it was a heartbeat, a defiant rhythm pounding through brownstone streets and trolley-lined avenues, a city within a city where baseball was gospel and Ebbets Field stood as its sacred temple. The faithful poured through its wrought-iron gates, a congregation in white and Dodger blue, waving scorecards like hymns, their voices rising in the immortal cadence of names that had long since become legends—Jackie Robinson, Duke Snider, Pee Wee Reese. Beneath those aging grandstands, fathers passed dreams to sons, the worn leather of their mitts carrying the weight of a thousand summers.

But time was a patient thief, stealing the years in whispers, eroding the edges of that old ballpark until its voice grew hoarse beneath the weight of progress. The wooden seats groaned against decades of devotion, the aisles too narrow for the crowds that still came, cheered, and clung to history. Brooklyn was changing, reshaping itself in the shadow of industry's retreat, as factories fell silent and families drifted toward the broad stretches of Long Island. The borough, once a stronghold of old-world pride, now teetered on the edge of reinvention, caught between past and future, between memory and necessity.

Walter O'Malley saw it all—felt it in every creaking plank and thinning crowd. He was not just a keeper of baseball but a steward of survival, and survival meant evolution. His quest to secure a new home for the Brooklyn Dodgers was a decade-long battle against an evolving urban landscape and the unyielding will of a single, powerful man. It was a fight for the soul of Brooklyn baseball, a struggle born from the aging grandeur of Ebbets Field, where parking was a logistical nightmare, limited to a paltry 700 cars scattered around the ballpark.

From the outset in 1946, O'Malley envisioned a privately financed, architecturally innovative domed stadium at the bustling intersection of Atlantic and Flatbush Avenues. He repeatedly clarified that he was not asking the city for a handout or a publicly funded stadium; he sought only the city's assistance in assembling the land, for which he, the ball club, would pay. His conviction, articulated in letters to figures like William Tracy, Vice Chairman of the Triborough Bridge and Tunnel Authority, was that the new ballpark should "occupy land on the tax roll," a striking contrast to the publicly funded stadiums emerging elsewhere in the nation. He even suggested that the mechanics of Title I of the 1949 Housing Act could be used if the ballpark also served as a parking garage, creating a dual-purpose civic benefit, including the potential to accommodate new passenger cars into Brooklyn via the Long Island Railroad depot, which would have further enhanced the area's connectivity.

His vision was ambitious, as detailed in correspondence with renowned engineers like Captain Emil Praeger, who, by October 22, 1946, already saw Brooklyn's urgent need for a larger stadium and even shared designs from a proposed memorial stadium for Washington, D.C. O'Malley also consulted with design luminaries like Norman Bel Geddes (whose 1948 study deemed renovation impractical due to continued parking issues).

Norman Bel Geddes-futurist was an early contributor to potential Dodger designs for a new stadium

Buckminster Fuller, and Eero Saarinen, (designer of the Gateway Arch in St. Louis) exploring the possibility of a 750-foot diameter translucent fiberglass shell. It wasn't merely a structural innovation; O'Malley saw "psychological reasons" in a translucent material to "properly set the stage for playing a traditionally outdoor game." He envisioned inverse hanging boxes instead of traditional upper tiers and a circular design for optimal lighting and views.

This provides clarity

Buckminster Fuller loved Geodesic Domes

He emphasized to Fuller, "I am not interested in just building another baseball park," highlighting his desire for a genuinely modern, weather-protected facility that would not only enhance the fan experience but also avoid costly rainouts and provide year-round uses for conventions and other events. The proposed 52,000-seat stadium, projected to cost $6 million, would have been the world's first domed stadium, predating Houston's Astrodome by a decade.

However, O'Malley's earnest appeals to New York City's powerful Parks Commissioner, Robert Moses, met with an impenetrable wall of resistance. Moses, a titan of urban planning, was reshaping New York with grand, sweeping infrastructure projects—expressways, bridges, and tunnels—prioritizing efficiency and vehicular traffic. He saw stadiums as utilitarian pieces in his vast urban puzzle, not as emotional landmarks integral to community identity. Not a baseball fan, Moses adamantly opposed O'Malley's preferred Brooklyn site. He viewed it as too congested, requiring significant changes to the subway system. He stubbornly pushed for a city-owned stadium in Flushing Meadows, Queens—a location that would later become Shea Stadium and Citi Field. To Moses, this was about logistics and regional accessibility; to O'Malley, it was about Brooklyn's soul.

This was his proposal for Walter O'Malley

The proposed Atlantic & Flatbush Avenues domed stadium from Colliers Magazine 1952

"Queens Dodgers" sounds like an awkward mismatch of history and geography—like calling the Statue of Liberty "Jersey's Torch." The Dodgers were Brooklyn's soul, deeply woven into the borough's culture, neighborhoods, and people. Rebranding them as belonging to Queens would have betrayed everything they stood for. Brooklyn fans were fiercely loyal, not just to the team but to the borough itself. They didn't cheer for the Dodgers simply because of the players—they cheered because the team was Brooklyn. The name "Brooklyn Dodgers" wasn't just a label; it was identity, courage, and heritage. It came from the days of trolley-dodging pedestrians, a symbol of working-class resilience. Uprooting them to Queens would have felt like stripping them of their essence, forcing them into a name that had no emotional resonance. Queens wasn't Brooklyn. It didn't have the same entrenched baseball history. It wasn't Ebbets Field. It wasn't the heart of a borough that bled Dodger blue. O'Malley knew this—he understood that a move to Queens would alienate the fans who had sustained the team for generations. That's why he fought for Brooklyn and envisioned a new stadium within its borders rather than accepting Robert Moses' push to relocate them to Queens. Had the team become the "Queens Dodgers," it likely wouldn't have survived in New York. The fanbase would have fractured, leaving the team stranded in a borough that never felt like home. Brooklyn would have mourned the loss just the same because once they left Ebbets Field, the team's heart went with them. In short, "Queens Dodgers" was never going to work. Brooklyn Dodgers? That was destiny. Queens Dodgers? That was a bureaucratic afterthought with no soul. O'Malley saw it, the fans knew it, and history proved that Brooklyn's baseball fate lay elsewhere.

The financial pressures on the team intensified beyond the prohibitive cost of land acquisition in a bustling, speculative market. In May 1954, O'Malley vehemently protested a new 5% admissions tax, warning Mayor Robert Wagner that it would make New York uncompetitive against other cities "ready to put money on the barrel head to get a major league baseball franchise." His telegram cited Baltimore, Milwaukee, Los Angeles, Dallas, Havana, Montreal, Toronto, Kansas City, and the Twin Cities as examples of aggressive suitors. Despite his urgent plea, the tax was implemented, costing the Dodgers a staggering $165,000 annually and contributing to overall federal and city taxes on admissions that reached nearly $500,000—more than the team's player payroll.

Faces say it all "no deal" O'Malley, Mayor Wagner, Stoneham, & Brooklyn Borough President Cashmore

Political delays compounded the challenges. Even with Governor Averell Harriman's public backing and the legislative creation of the Brooklyn Sports Center Authority, the project became mired in bureaucratic inertia. Moses's influence loomed large; his internal memos declared the Atlantic Avenue site "dead" and persistently advocated for Flushing Meadow. In his internal memorandum, O'Malley characterized Moses's actions as "a further bit of sabotage" and lamented the lack of "sincere administration desire to work out a solution here in Brooklyn."

The final attempts to keep the Dodgers in Brooklyn proved futile. A proposal by City Council President Abe Stark to rebuild the Ebbets Field site with expanded parking was summarily rejected by both O'Malley and

Moses. Even a last-ditch effort by financier Nelson Rockefeller in September to acquire land for a stadium, which grew to a $3 million offer and included the idea of a rent-free lease for 20 years, was ultimately deemed too expensive by O'Malley. He clarified to Mayor Wagner that such a price "priced the Dodgers out." At the time, Rockefeller, a political newcomer with gubernatorial ambitions, was viewed by O'Malley with some suspicion, seeing his involvement as potentially transparent posturing rather than a genuine commitment to keeping the team in Brooklyn. On January 10, 1955, Columnist Tommy Holmes of the Brooklyn Eagle spoke to Walter O'Malley on the hope of building a new stadium in Brooklyn. O'Malley said, "We have explored all of Brooklyn and have considered every location which might be considered appropriate desirable". On January 19, 1955, Columnist Jimmy Powers of the New York Daily News interviewed Walter O'Malley who talked of the need for a new baseball stadium to replace aging Ebbets Field. "We want the government to approve slum clearance plans in neighborhoods which would be suitable for a new ballpark. Then we could build the park which would have the capacity, transportation and parking facilities to make the new Ebbets Field a valuable addition to our city".

With all the avenues in Brooklyn exhausted and Moses unyielding, O'Malley had to consider other options. The National League's unanimous consent for the Dodgers and Giants to move to Los Angeles and San Francisco solidified the potential for relocation. To shore up capital for land and construction costs for a new stadium, O'Malley even sold his ballpark in Montreal (then a Triple-A affiliate) before the move. Having previously engaged with Los Angeles officials who were eager to embrace major league baseball, O'Malley found a receptive audience. The Los Angeles City Council officially adopted an ordinance inviting the Dodgers, outlining a contract that obligated O'Malley to privately finance and build a 50,000-seat stadium, develop a youth recreation center with an initial investment of $500,000 plus annual payments of $60,000 for 20 years, and pay property taxes on previously untaxed land—initially estimated at $345,000 annually. The Dodgers would also transfer team-owned Wrigley Field in Los Angeles, appraised at $2.25 million, to the city; this ballpark would notably serve as the home field for the Los Angeles Angels of the American League in 1961. It was a commitment that stood in stark contrast to the bureaucratic stalemates and financial disincentives in New York.

Walter O'Malley met with Nelson Rockefeller, but it was too little too late and at that point Rockefeller was a new, unknown factor that could not be relied on.

Even as O'Malley pressed forward, political delays mounted. The Brooklyn Sports Center Authority, formed to oversee stadium construction, became ensnared in legislative bottlenecks, unable to cut through the red tape needed to secure land. Time was slipping away, and O'Malley knew it. Frustration turned to ink, O'Malley's hand steady as he wrote his vision into history, a plea not for funding but for freedom—to build, dream, and carve a future where baseball could last. But the forces aligned against him showed no signs of compromise. Even as Brooklyn fought its bureaucratic battle, another team—the New York Giants—found itself at a crossroads. Horace Stoneham had initially planned to relocate his franchise to Minneapolis, where he would disband his Triple-A affiliate and start fresh. But O'Malley saw things differently. He understood that baseball's future wasn't merely about moving teams—it was about sustaining rivalries, maintaining competitive balance, and ensuring the survival of the National League's identity. Air travel had erased the logistical barriers of cross-country scheduling, making West Coast expansion more viable than ever. So, O'Malley convinced Stoneham to abandon Minneapolis and join him on an entirely new frontier: San Francisco. All this was finally decided during a hunting trip to Wyoming.

The negotiation session between Chad McClellan and Walter O'Malley took place in Rawlins, Wyoming during the first week of September 1957. It was during this meeting that tensions rose significantly between the two parties. McClellan expressed his frustration openly, stating, "I was angry with his (O'Malley) indecisiveness," and firmly told O'Malley, "I told him that what we had offered was the best we could do."

Following his return from Wyoming, McClellan made a stop in Denver, Colorado. While there, he wrote a letter to O'Malley using Trans World Airlines stationery, which read: "Dear Walter: I'm sorry we didn't have more time together—perhaps we did clear up a few points. Enclosed you will find a brief outline of the alternative suggestion I offered in trying to find a practical solution. I thought you might like to have this prior to calling me Tuesday. Regards, Chad McClellan."

After receiving the letter, O'Malley contacted McClellan by phone two days later, signaling the beginning of the final phase of the negotiation. The deal points began to narrow, leading to O'Malley ultimately accepting the offer from the city of Los Angeles. He agreed to relocate the Dodgers

ALLEN SCHERY

and construct Dodger Stadium—a venue where the team continues to play more than six decades later.

McClellan later reflected on the impact of the successful negotiation and the long-term benefits it brought to Los Angeles. He stated, "The benefits our city and county have derived defy description. Millions upon millions of dollars flow into our community yearly from payrolls, visitor purchases, hotel accommodations, restaurant patronage and general economic activity. Taxes are generated on many, many transactions aside from property assessment. Trains, planes, autos and charter buses bring visitors from far and near. Youngsters everywhere have new, wholesome recreation available—and they like it."

Brooklyn's loss to the Dodgers wasn't just a sports story; it mirrored the tectonic shifts across postwar America. The 1940s and '50s were a time of rapid urban transformation, with suburban expansion, highway construction, and changing economic centers altering the fabric of many cities. Dwight D. Eisenhower's Interstate Highway System was one of American history's most transformative infrastructure projects. The Federal-Aid Highway Act, signed into law on June 29, 1956, created a vast network of controlled-access highways designed for efficiency, defense, and economic growth. However, this also added to potential future turmoil. Once a powerhouse of industry, Brooklyn witnessed the retreat of manufacturing and the rise of suburban migration as families moved to Long Island and beyond. The potential relocation of the Dodgers was emblematic of this future transition; what once made Brooklyn vibrant and self-sustaining was now giving way to a more dispersed metropolitan existence. Infrastructure projects like Robert Moses' massive highway expansions fundamentally reshaped communities. The preference for automobiles over public transit reflected a new vision of urban planning, prioritizing accessibility to growing suburban areas rather than reinforcing the density of traditional city centers. In many ways, O'Malley's battle wasn't just about baseball; it was about the fight between an old, neighborhood-centric urban model and the sprawling, automobile-driven future Moses championed.

One thing never mentioned in all this is that Walter O'Malley's entire essence was New York. Whether it be the Bronx, Hollis, Amityville, Brooklyn, his wife and children, business associates, and a decade-long proven track record of trying to keep the Dodgers in Brooklyn, and his love for fishing in nearby waters. How likely would it be that he pull a red herring like Los Angeles out of his hat? All the discourse and false narrative hinged only on one thing—his refusal to accept Flushing Meadows as an alternative for his new home. Once, New York power broker Robert Moses had that soundbite he kept pounding the table with it. It finally became cemented in the minds of locals with the birth of the New York Mets, and Shea Stadium in the same Flushing Meadows O'Malley turned down. The assuming of the Dodgers and Giants colors for the Mets was the last nail in this erstwhile coffin. Meanwhile, through all this, Walter O'Malley was 3000 miles away and too busy to be involved in a one-sided conversation.

And yet, even as Brooklyn faded from the Dodgers' future, O'Malley was already laying the foundation for something new. Dodgertown, the team's Vero Beach, Florida, spring training facility, was another testament to his vision. In 1952, Emil Praeger, the same engineer who had dreamed up Brooklyn's future stadium, submitted construction estimates for a 5,000-seat stadium in Vero Beach. Dodgertown was more than a training ground—it was a baseball sanctuary. In this place, the Dodgers could refine their craft, away from the political battles and bureaucratic entanglements of New York.

Time stands still for no one! Here is a model of Dodger Stadium (L-R) Capt. Emil Praeger, designer; Walter O'Malley; Al Vinnell of Vinnell Constructors; James Mulvey, Dodger Vice President and stockholder; Jack Yount of Vinnell Constructors and on-site construction manager; and Dick Walsh, Dodger Vice President, Stadium Operations.

The fight for Brooklyn's baseball soul was slipping into its final innings, the clock ticking toward a future neither borough nor ballpark could outrun. The Dodgers still played beneath the aging beams of Ebbets Field, but its foundation trembled—not from the weight of history, but from the forces aligning beyond its gates. Walter O'Malley had spent years pushing against immovable obstacles, the ink of his letters drying before they could bend New York's bureaucratic machine. Politicians' promises were fading echoes, drowned out by Robert Moses's rigid resolve, whose vision of urban efficiency saw no place for sentiment or baseball. The great chess match between them had stretched for a decade, but now the pieces were nearing their final moves. Even within the Dodgers' clubhouse, whispers were growing. The players could feel the uncertainty, the tension, the quiet realization that the future wouldn't wait for Brooklyn to catch up. O'Malley wasn't merely chasing a stadium anymore; he was chasing survival, carving out a path where baseball could endure beyond the crumbling facades of Ebbets Field. And yet, despite the looming inevitability, Brooklyn's "faithful" still filled the stands, cheered, and clung to the hope that history was too sacred to be rewritten. They waved their scorecards like prayer books, their voices rising into the night air, unaware that they were witnesses to the final summer of Brooklyn baseball as they knew it. For now, the Dodgers were still there. But the cracks beneath them were growing and soon would become a chasm.

And so, history unfolded exactly as Moses had planned.

The Dodgers' final season in Brooklyn carried the weight of a runaway train. Fans packed Ebbets Field one last time, gripping the splintered wooden seats, holding on to the hope that something, anything, might prevent the inevitable. But the inevitable came, and the gates closed forever.

Brooklyn mourned. Bars shut down, businesses folded, and neighborhoods felt as if they had lost a vital part of their spirit. The echoes of a stadium once alive with cheers, chants, and heartbreak faded into silence.

Dodgers star Carl Furillo captured the borough's sorrow in a single statement.

"The kids are the ones who will suffer the most."

Ebbets Field stood abandoned, a monument to a lost civilization. The grandstands withered under the weight of time, rust covering the once-polished steel. The scoreboard, once flashing with excitement, now stood frozen and lifeless. Weeds pushed through cracks in the pavement, reclaiming a ballpark that had been discarded by the city that once worshipped it.

By 1960, Ebbets Field was erased, demolished without ceremony. There was no farewell, no tribute, just wrecking balls swinging through history, reducing Brooklyn's baseball cathedral to rubble and dust.

Then came the final irony.

In 2012, the land O'Malley had fought for, the land Moses had refused to grant for baseball, became home to Barclays Center, a modern arena built for Brooklyn Nets basketball. Not for baseball. Not for the Dodgers.

Brooklynites never forgot. The betrayal could still be felt in the borough's streets, in the conversations of aging fans who still wore their Brooklyn Dodgers caps, refusing to let go of a past stolen from them.

The same question still haunts history. If this land was good enough for basketball, why wasn't it good enough for baseball?

But perhaps the Dodgers' departure was more than just a tragedy—it was a turning point in the story of America itself.

From the birth of the nation, the United States had always looked westward. The original thirteen colonies, clustered along the Eastern Seaboard, saw their destiny beyond the Appalachian Mountains, beyond the Mississippi River, beyond the unknown frontier. Lewis and Clark carved the first path through the uncharted wilds, opening the door for settlers, dreamers, and pioneers. California, isolated from the rest of the country, became a state in 1850, standing alone, waiting for the rest of America to reach its shores.

Baseball, the game that grew alongside the nation, mirrored this trajectory. By the mid-20th century, the major leagues had sixteen teams, all packed into the dense cities of the East and Midwest. There was no presence south of Washington, D.C., no franchises beyond St. Louis or Chicago. The game remained tethered to its historical strongholds, unwilling to step into the vast expanse that stretched toward the Pacific.

Walter O'Malley and Horace Stoneham changed that forever.

Like Lewis and Clark pushing into the unknown, O'Malley and Stoneham led baseball's own expedition west. Their teams, the Dodgers and Giants, set forth into territory untouched by Major League Baseball, bridging the great divide between the Mississippi River and California. They weren't just relocating, they were trailblazers, expanding the sport's borders in a way no one else dared.

For Brooklyn, it was heartbreak. For baseball, it was inevitable.

The game had reached a moment of transformation, where it could either remain bound to the past or embrace the promise of the future. O'Malley

ALLEN SCHERY

and Stoneham saw the future. Their move west wasn't just a business decision—it was a continuation of Manifest Destiny itself.

Baseball, like America, had finally conquered the frontier.

Final summary based on truth not soundbites

Walter O'Malley's extensive search for a new home for the Brooklyn Dodgers between 1946 and 1957 involved considering numerous sites across New York City, driven by the severe inadequacies of an aging Ebbets Field in Flatbush, which suffered from limited parking and deteriorating conditions. Initially, O'Malley explored renovating or rebuilding Ebbets Field itself, but studies quickly deemed this unfeasible and too expensive. His primary and most consistent vision centered on a privately financed, 52,000-seat domed stadium at the highly accessible intersection of Atlantic and Flatbush Avenues in Fort Greene, Brooklyn, a site chosen for its unparalleled public transit access via nine subway lines and the Long Island Railroad terminal. This ambitious plan, however, faced staunch opposition from New York City Construction Coordinator, kingpin Robert Moses, who cited complex land acquisition, potential tax revenue loss, and unspecified "significant changes to the New York City Subway system" as reasons for his rejection, rooted in a philosophical clash over public (Moses) versus private (O'Malley) ownership. On September 17, 1955, The New York Daily News wrote an editorial following a series of articles by reporter Robert Stearns of issues facing significant congestion from the Fort Greene Meat Market. The editorial stated, "The Long Island station at Atlantic Ave., one of the busiest terminals in town, can't handle the newest and longest coaches because its present tracks are so curlicued. The Fort Greene Market, strangled by traffic congestion is a buyer's bedlam. If it were relocated in a more logical Brooklyn area, our borough's retailers and wholesalers would cheer, and our housewives would save from one to five cents per pound on their meat budgets. The spot would make a perfect location for a new Dodgers ballpark".

Beyond his preferred Atlantic and Flatbush site, O'Malley and other proponents explored numerous and unending alternatives within Brooklyn. In March 1948, a report by Emil Praeger of Madigan & Hyland identified an "extremely desirable site" in the Downtown District, bound by Myrtle Avenue, Ashland Place, Lafayette Street, and Fleet Street, as suitable for a modern stadium. The Dodger Board of Directors also authorized O'Malley to explore the Borough Hall section of Brooklyn in February 1948 as a potential site. Other proposals came from external parties: the Coney Island Chamber of Commerce offered the former Luna Park site by the boardwalk, but it did not meet O'Malley's criteria for a modern, transit-and parking-oriented major league venue. Similarly, City Council President Abe Stark offered The Parade Ground in Brooklyn, but this faced significant public opposition and legal hurdles regarding the use of public parkland for a private entity. In July 1956, consulting engineers Clarke and Rapuano proposed a stadium on the south side of Flatbush Avenue bordering Fourth and Prospect in Park Slope as part of a broader urban renewal project, distinct from O'Malley's preferred Atlantic Terminal site, but this also met with Robert Moses's differing opinions and ultimate preference for the Atlantic Terminal area or Flushing Meadows. Another site mentioned in the O'Malley files and seen nowhere else has historical significance. It was located at 4th and 5th Avenue between 17th and 20th Streets and was about a dozen blocks from the team's very first location, Washington Park 1 which was located at 4th and 5th Avenues between 3rd and 5th Avenues. O'Malley faced the same issues as the original owners as the land had a 30-foot "slope" to it. This should not be surprising as it would have been in the Park Slope area of Brooklyn. According to a TIME magazine article dated April 28th, 1958 entitled "Walter in Wonderland Walter stated: Other sites were mentioned including "'one between a cemetery and Jamaica Bay" O'Malley quickly retorted, "...we weren't likely to get many customers from either place."

Robert Moses consistently and frustratingly countered O'Malley's Brooklyn plans by advocating for a city-owned stadium in Flushing Meadows, Queens, a site that eventually became home to Shea Stadium. O'Malley, however, rejected Flushing Meadows due to concerns about the loss of the Dodgers' Brooklyn identity, the site's geographic isolation (surrounded by water and cemeteries), and his doubt that the neighborhood could sustain a major league team. This insistence by Moses on Flushing Meadows, coupled with his declaration in August 1957 that the Atlantic Avenue site was "dead," was viewed by O'Malley as "sabotage" and a clear indication that no solution would be worked out in Brooklyn. To exert pressure on New York City, O'Malley strategically played temporary "home" games at Roosevelt Stadium in Jersey City during the 1956 and 1957 seasons, though this was never intended as a permanent relocation.

Walter O'Malley's extensive files also contain various mentions. The research does not indicate that "Horace Harding and Junction," "Carleton Avenue Yards," or "Fort Greene Place" and "Horace Harding and Queens Blvd" locations were distinct stadium sites he formally explored for the Brooklyn Dodgers, but they do indicate O'Malley's undying efforts to leave no stone unturned to stay in New York.

If there is still any doubt of O'Malley's intent to stay in Brooklyn there is yet another letter in the O'Malley archival files dated February 11th, 1954, to Frank Schroth of the Brooklyn Eagle regarding a Long Island City site over the Railroad yards never seen in print before stating that "A move to Long Island City would be preferred to Los Angeles".

The author can attest to even further conversations regarding Brooklyn Union Gas properties. The author's aunt, Marion Schery, worked for the aforementioned gas company at 195 Montague Street throughout this era as personnel director. The Dodgers' main office was two buildings away at 215 Montague Street. Both Judge Henry Ughetta (who was appointed by George V. McLaughlin to help guide O'Malley) and O'Malley were on the board of directors of the Dodgers and Brooklyn Union Gas; The Dodgers' office was located in the Mechanics' Savings Bank and is where Jackie Robinson signed his historic contract. Both Truman Capote and W.E.B. Du Bois called this Brooklyn Heights area (right near the Brooklyn Bridge) their home. Marion Schery was a close friend of Ughetta's and spent many holidays at Marion Schery's house in nearby Richmond Hill. The author overheard many stories of possible Dodger relocations to various and sundry Brooklyn Union Gas sites.

Ergo, any of the myriad stories that even today still float in the ether are either the result of errant reporting or the human tendency to gather sound bites using confirmation bias. To prove this, I will close this section to help future researchers by saying there is no stitch of evidence of Gerritsen Beach or Staten Island proposals. The first would have had flooding issues and the second would assume people crossing the Verrazano Bridge from Brooklyn. This is something the working-class people from the "city of churches" would not have done. The only stitch of evidence regarding a Staten Island site is the following: On August 22, 1955 – The Staten Island Advance wrote a story that a Staten Island councilman asked Mayor Robert Wagner of New York City if there was any consideration to build a baseball stadium on the island. A New York State Assemblyman Lucio F. Russo wrote a letter to Walter O'Malley that, "Forget about moving to New Jersey but to come to the Island where you will find all the land you need for baseball and parking."

Chapter Fifteen
Ebbets Field's End and Brooklyn's Loss (1958-1960s)

In the languid twilight of a bygone era, Brooklyn bore witness to a farewell that shook its soul. The once-mighty Ebbets Field—an exalted sanctuary where dreams and heroics intertwined like the delicate petals of a rare flower—succumbed to the inexorable force of progress. It happened with a precision that was both awe-inspiring and heartbreakingly clinical, as bulldozers and heavy machinery, like monstrous beasts, devoured the sacred coliseum of baseball lore, reducing it to mere fragments of rubble. Every weathered brick, once pulsating with the electric breath of cheering crowds and impassioned legends, now lay scattered like relics of a lost age, each a tiny, silent monument evoking a mosaic of shining memories and lingering echoes. In the whispers of the wind that swept through the space where grandeur once stood, one could almost hear the mellifluous chants and triumphant roars of Dodgers fans—a timeless chorus memorializing moments when every spirited summer night at Ebbets Field resonated with unbridled passion and communal pride, a symphony of joy now reduced to a mournful sigh.

Within the rich tapestry of Brooklyn's history, personal vignettes have survived the relentless march of time, breathing life into the spectral memory of Ebbets Field like flickering candles against a deepening twilight. Hilda Chester whose eyes glowed with the bittersweet luminescence of faded summers, recalled with tearful ardor how her youthful mornings were spent on sun-warmed stoops, her small heart transfixed by the distant cadence of cheering that emanated from those hallowed grounds. "You could feel it; you could feel the game even blocks away," she would whisper, her voice thick with unshed tears, "like the whole neighborhood was breathing together." Similarly, the recollections of Jimmy—a rugged son of Brooklyn whose soul still shimmered with the sparkle of forgotten tournaments played on dusty sandlots, fueled by dreams of one day gracing that very field—stood as storied testimonies to baseball brilliance and neighborhood kinship. Their cherished anecdotes, delicately rendered in hues of nostalgia and reverence, woven with the thread of a profound, collective heartbreak, transformed everyday street corners and rain-slick alleys into living monuments of an era when the field was sacrosanct and every game a grand celebration of hope, a vibrant thread in the very fabric of their lives, now tragically unraveled.

BROOKLYN DODGERS AT EBBETS FIELD 1913-1957

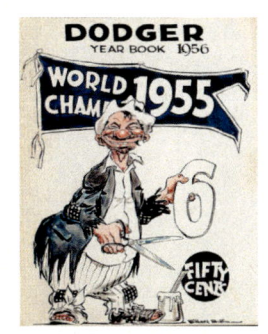

1956 Brooklyn Dodgers Yearbook from Author's Dodger Museum Collection "Bum" artwork by Willard Mullins

The demolition of Ebbets Field marked not merely the physical annihilation of brick and mortar but the rupture of Brooklyn's spirit. This seismic transformation cleaved tradition from progress, leaving a gaping wound where a thriving heart once beat. As monumental walls tumbled and dust swirled like lost memories dancing upon the wind, the jubilant voices of a community were hushed into quiet lament, replaced by the grating roar of machines. The departure of the Dodgers, those indomitable icons of valor and unity, those "Bums" who were unequivocally theirs, left an aching void. In this chasm, collective memory and communal pride converged into a silent, unfilled absence. It was as if a beloved family member had vanished, leaving behind only the echoing silence of their absence. Nevertheless, even in that profound loss lay the fertile ground of metamorphosis, as Brooklyn, like a heartbroken phoenix, began to channel its grief into a bold reimagining of self and space, refusing to be defined solely by what it had lost.

Amid this complex interplay of mourning and modernity, Brooklyn seemed to adopt a poetic cadence—a measured, almost musical recollection of its illustrious past interlaced with the vibrant pulse of fresh beginnings, a slow, aching melody of resilience. The borough's urban fabric became a living canvas where the patina of time, with its warm, amber hues of decay and renewal, softly brushed against the sharp lines of contemporary design. Murals sprang up on timeworn walls, each stroke a tribute to the indomitable legacy of Ebbets Field, vibrant echoes of the past painted against the backdrop of a changing future. At the same time, the echo of legendary cheers found its way into the lyrics of local ballads and the murmur of sidewalk conversations, woven into the very rhythm of daily life. In these harmonies of past and present, Brooklyn's citizens fashioned a resilient narrative—one in which loss was but the prologue to an ever-unfolding saga of hope, a poignant testament to the unbreakable spirit of a community that had known profound joy and devastating sorrow.

Seamlessly intertwined with this resilient revival was a newfound cultural renaissance from the crucible of grief. Bearing the weight of shared memory, Brooklyn's artists, poets, and musicians began to excavate the depths of that collective sorrow, transforming the bittersweet remnants of the demolished stadium into creative allegories. Sidewalks became open-air galleries displaying ephemeral installations inspired by the legacy of the Dodgers, each piece a whispered conversation with a cherished ghost. At the same time, beloved ballads and impassioned verses recited in neighborhood cafes recalled the echoes of a fabled summer past, their melodies infused with a nostalgic ache. Each mural, each song, and every whispered story in the shadowed corners of the borough was imbued with the timeless spirit of Ebbets Field. This spirit transcended physicality to ignite the imaginative flame in hearts, young and old, a quiet promise that the memories would never truly fade

18 of Author's PM-10 Dodger pins sold exclusively at Ebbets Field, worn on Author's T-Shirt

In quiet, introspective moments beneath a mellow sunset, as the last rays of light bathed the Brooklyn skyline in a golden glow, Brooklyn's spirit found itself inexorably intertwined with the fabled past of Ebbets Field. As neighborhoods matured and the modern pulse of urban life grew ever stronger, the memory of each game played and every heroic feat executed on those sacred grounds transformed into a cherished allegory—an eternal dialogue between impermanence and endurance. The demolition, an act of both sorrow and rebirth, was not simply an end but a transformative denouement that ushered in an era where loss nurtured a powerful vision for renewal. In its most transcendent form, it became a metaphoric crucible where the embers of memory, though painful, fueled the bright flames of hope and reinvention, proving that even the most profound endings can pave the way for beautiful new beginnings.

Thus, dear reader, allow yourself to be drawn into the reverie of Brooklyn's hallowed past. In that past, every celebrated cheer and every tearful goodbye conspired to forge an everlasting legacy, a diamond dust shimmering in the collective consciousness. The elegiac strains of Ebbets Field persist, not just in dusty archives or fading photographs, but in the whispering winds that rustle through brownstone stoops, the murmuring streets alive with new dreams, and the radiant glances of those whose eyes still reflect the glory of a time when baseball was not merely a game but an epic narrative of passion, community, and soul. In the reflective twilight of remembrance, Brooklyn invites each soul to explore the delicate interplay between the splendor of memory and the audacious promise of tomorrow, a promise whispered with the tender hope of a fresh start.

In the luminous interplay of shadow and light, where every fragment of memory dances with the pulse of modern ambition, Brooklyn emerges as an enduring canvas—a tribute to a past that, though physically dispersed, remains indelibly etched upon the hearts of its people, a scar of love. The borough continues its timeless dialogue with history amid the vibrant murmur of rejuvenated streets and the persistent call of old legends. It is a conversation that spans generations, capturing the relentless spirit of those who once roared beneath the skies of Ebbets Field, their voices echoing in the very foundations, and those who now breathe new vitality into every corner of this transformative urban realm, building upon the hallowed ground that once was.

Thus, in this exquisite nexus of grief and grandeur, the story of Ebbets Field and the enduring legacy of the Dodgers is not confined to the annals of sports history; it is woven, thread by thread, into the fabric of Brooklyn's collective identity. Each cobblestone, each meticulously preserved facade, and every repurposed mural stands as a testament to a community that dares to cherish its past, to feel the ache of its losses while simultaneously embracing the bold, resplendent promise of the future. In celebrating the bittersweet loss and the invigorating birth of a new chapter, Brooklyn remains a luminous beacon, forever echoing the immortal strains of a bygone era and inspiring the dreamers of tomorrow. This city learned to heal, remember, and carry its heartbreak with a defiant, beautiful grace.

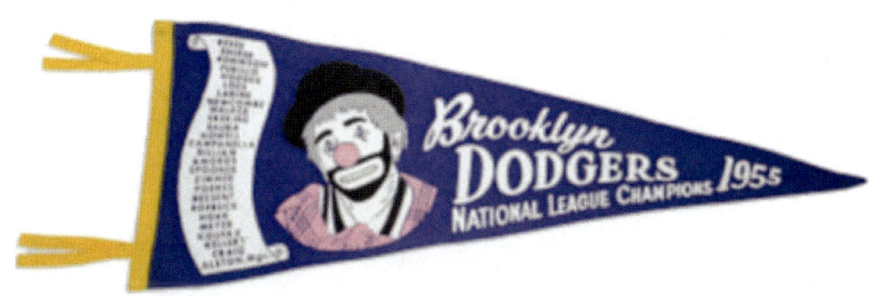

1955 Brooklyn Dodger Pennant from Author's Dodger Museum Collection.

Chapter Sixteen
The Last Season at Ebbets Field – A Farewell to Brooklyn (1957)

Then came the summer of 1957, the final act in a grand, bittersweet saga that had defined Brooklyn baseball for 45 illustrious seasons. Ebbets Field, that hallowed stage where heroes danced and dreams took flight, now bore the heavy weight of an impending farewell. Its weathered seats and ivy-clad walls, steeped in countless triumphs and heartbreaks, seemed to whisper memories of glory to the cool, clear September air tinged with melancholy. The very atmosphere carried the scent of wet concrete and nostalgia—a poignant reminder of golden days when every game ignited hope in the hearts of a loyal congregation. The cries of vendors hawking peanuts and programs, the crack of the bat, the roar of the crowd – all these sounds, once so vibrant, now resonated with an underlying current of finality.

Throughout that fateful season, the Dodgers fought with the same relentless, defiant spirit that had long enchanted the faithful. They compiled an admirable 84–70 record, a tribute to their enduring grit even as whispers of relocation and the pressures of a shifting baseball landscape drifted like autumn leaves across every dugout and bleacher. Owner Walter O'Malley's decade-long, impassioned struggle to secure a new stadium for a dying Brooklyn echoed like an unspoken elegy amidst the clamor of uncertainty. He battled against political inertia and financial constraints, his vision of a modern stadium for his beloved team constantly thwarted. Even as several home games were shifted to Roosevelt Stadium in Jersey City—a temporary stand-in that only deepened the sense of inevitable loss, a stark reminder of what was to come—the soul of Ebbets Field remained unbowed, a monument to the immortal spirit of Brooklyn baseball. The move, intended to showcase a potential future, only served to highlight the irreplaceable charm of the Dodgers' true home.

1957 Topps Danny McDevitt-winning pitcher of last game played at Ebbets Field from Author's Dodger Museum Collection.

The final game at this iconic park came on September 24, 1957—a swan song for a cherished era. On that cool evening, as 6,702 ardent fans gathered in a hushed, reflective crowd, their faces etched with a mixture of sorrow and reverence, the Dodgers wrapped up their storied tenure in Brooklyn with a 2–0 victory over the Pittsburgh Pirates. In a measured and magnificent performance, veteran pitcher Danny McDevitt ascended to the mound and delivered a masterful complete game. Allowing only five hits while striking out nine batters, McDevitt's display was a crystalline embodiment of the grit and determination that had long been the hallmark of the Boys of Summer. With every pitch, the game's 2–0 scoreline resonated not merely as a numerical triumph but as a bittersweet acknowledgment that history was, inexorably, turning its page. Each out brought the finality closer, each run a memory to be cherished.

In those final moments, the familiar, rasping baritone of Tex Rickards—the voice that had once announced countless thrilling contests, whose pronouncements had become an integral part of the Ebbets Field experience—echoed across the field one last time. Legendary figures such as Pee Wee Reese, Gil Hodges, and Roy Campanella moved with a quiet, dignified grace, their every play imbued with sparkling memories of past glories and the subtle sorrow of impending departure. Their movements, normally so fluid and powerful, now carried an unspoken weight. Even the iconic Bull Durham sign on the right-field fence, long a herald of commerce and community, stood silently as if to bid adieu to an entire generation for whom Ebbets Field had been sacred, its painted bull a silent witness to decades of baseball magic.

Ebbets Field game day announcer Tex Rickards from Author's Dodger Museum Collection.

Yet, amid the somber farewells, the final season at Ebbets Field was also a rousing celebration—a defiant salute to decades of passion, perseverance, and unyielding love for the game. Every stolen base, every gravity-defying catch, every powerful swing was a verse in the eternal hymn of Brooklyn baseball. The air seemed to vibrate with an unscripted symphony, where the crowd's roar mingled with the clanging of makeshift instruments in the stands. At the heart of this living orchestra was the indomitable Howlin' Hilda Chester—a beacon of unwavering fan devotion whose impassioned shouts and the resonant clang of her brass cowbell rallied the faithful, her presence as much a part of Ebbets Field as the players themselves. Alongside her, the Dodgers Symphony—a motley, joyous band led in its earliest days by Carmine "Shorty" Laurice and later by the stalwart Lou "Brother Lou" Soriano, with the piercing whistle of Eddie Bettan punctuating every crescendo—lent an irreverent, yet deeply stirring accompaniment to the spectacle on the diamond, their music a testament to the enduring joy found within those walls.

Hilda Chester was a fixture at Ebbets Field. Her voice and cowbell were unforgettable.

ALLEN SCHERY

The Sym-phony Band was really bad. They used to walk through the neighborhood playing their bottom ten music, upsetting grandmothers and pets alike. They claimed they were practicing! -- proving that practice does not make poifect.

Thus, as the season's golden light waned beneath the dimming floodlights and the final cheers gave way to a reflective silence, Ebbets Field transcended its physical form to become a repository of dreams—a museum of memories forever etched into the heart of America's favorite pastime. The Dodgers' last season in Brooklyn emerged as an indelible chapter in the annals of baseball history—a time of poignant goodbyes, triumphant moments, and an enduring legacy that sings the eternal hymn of Brooklyn's immortal spirit. Even as time marches on, and new stadiums rise, the echoes of that vibrant symphony of heroic plays, tearful farewells, and the steadfast roar of a community united continue to reverberate, ensuring that the magic of Ebbets Field lives on in every cherished remembrance. The little kids cried and did not understand what had happened. Or why. They would speak about it for years, wearing their Brooklyn Dodger hats as a silent, enduring tribute to their loss, a generation forever marked by the bittersweet memory of a team and a home that were, for a fleeting moment, utterly their own.

Chapter Seventeen
Remembering Ebbets Field and the Brooklyn Dodgers

Ebbets Field may have vanished from the Brooklyn skyline, a cruel erasure of beloved history. However, its legacy endures a vibrant, aching phantom in the hearts of those who lived and breathed baseball during its storied existence. To many, it was more than merely a ballpark—it was a cherished monument, a neighborhood temple where every worn brick and creaking wooden seat testified to the glory, the strife, and the soul-stirring beauty of the game. In that intimate arena, the Brooklyn Dodgers transcended the label of a mere team to embody a borough's resilient spirit, shaping identities and infusing everyday life with hope and purpose. For generations, the stadium was the thumping heart of Brooklyn, and its loss left an echo that still resonates, a silent ache in the borough's soul.

BROOKLYN DODGERS AT EBBETS FIELD 1913-1957

Cookie Lavagetto's double broke up a near-perfect game in the 1947 World Series

Within the hallowed walls of Ebbets Field, history was forged in moments that ranged from the quietly revolutionary to high-drama spectacles, each etched into collective memory with the precision of a master engraver. Beyond the day when Jackie Robinson, with unyielding courage in the face of hatred, first stepped onto the diamond, forever altering baseball's destiny and the very fabric of American society, the park bore witness to feats of daring and brilliance that now read like chapters in a myth. There was the unforgettable day when Cookie Lavagetto's miraculous double broke up a near-perfect game in the 1947 World Series. A sudden, explosive burst of joy sent a shockwave of delight through Dodgers fans, leaving their rivals in stunned disbelief. Carl Erskine's display of pitching mastery—his record-setting 14 strikeouts in a single series game—resonated as a tribute to Brooklyn's never-say-die attitude, echoing like a defiant call through the corridors of time.

October 2nd, 1953, Carl Erskine sets the World Series record by striking out 14 Yankees. Photo from Author's Dodger Museum Collection.

The final game played on September 24, 1957, encapsulated the bittersweet end of an era, a final, heartbreaking performance. On that cool autumn afternoon, with the weight of impending loss evident in the eyes of every devoted fan—each tear that welled a silent testament to the grief that clung to the air—Danny McDevitt took the mound with a calm determination. Pitching a complete-game shutout against the Pittsburgh Pirates, he allowed only five hits. He struck out nine batters, securing a 2-0 victory for the Dodgers in a farewell that was as tender as valiant, a poignant last dance. In that game, every play bore the significance of finality. With timely and resolute swings, Gil Hodges and Elmer Valo drove in the crucial runs that signaled Brooklyn's undying defiance, a final, defiant roar in the face of inevitable silence. Furthermore, in a moment heavy with triumph and despair, Gino Cimoli scored the final run ever recorded at Ebbets Field—a symbolic culmination of decades of glory and the agonizing passing of a cherished chapter.

Gino Cimoli scored the last Brooklyn Dodger run. He was traded for Wally Moon the following year. 1957 Topps card # 379 from Author's Dodger Museum Collection.

Brooklyn's infatuation with baseball was inescapable, woven into the fabric of daily life, as essential as the air they breathed. The Dodgers were not merely a team; they were a way of life, an emblem of the hopes, struggles, and steadfast pride of a people who found solace and identity in each game. On hot summer nights and brisk autumn afternoons, the voices of Brooklynites—ringing from street corners, reverberating in neighborhood diners, and passed down in lively barbershop conversations—celebrated every stolen base and every daring play as if their own lives hung in the balance. The legendary rivalry with the Yankees transcended mere competition; it was a cultural clash of identities, pitting Brooklyn's raw, gritty heart against the perceived refinement and prestige of another borough's power. In every retelling, the Dodgers' victories were as much about community, defiance, and the underdog's triumph as they were about the game itself, a fierce, protective love for their "Bums."

The impact of Ebbets Field extends beyond memory and the echo of past cheers—it has also sculpted the modern architecture of baseball, a ghostly blueprint for future generations. The intimate seating and the unique quirks of the park's design—the short right-field wall that transformed routine fly balls into legendary home runs and the narrow concourses that forced fans into close communion with the players—set a standard that many modern ballparks strive to emulate. Today, stadiums such as Camden Yards and Coors Field echo that ethos, favoring proximity and character over the sterile vastness of multi-purpose arenas, attempting to recapture lost magic. Each modern venue, in its own way, seeks to capture the thrill of being close to the action, the electrifying sensation of hearing every crack of the bat, much like the golden days when Ebbets Field was the pulsating nucleus of baseball society.

No contemporary park more explicitly pays tribute to that bygone era than Citi Field, home of the New York Mets, born from the longing for what was lost. Designed with a reverence for tradition, Citi Field's brick façade, arched entryways, and especially the Jackie Robinson Rotunda stand as direct, loving homages to Ebbets Field, a bridge between grief and remembrance. Fred Wilpon, a Brooklyn native, ensured that every element of Citi Field's design resonated with echoes of the past, infusing modernity with the timeless charm of the classic ballpark that once defined baseball in Brooklyn. Here, visitors are invited to step into a space equipped with contemporary amenities and a portal to history—a tangible bridge linking today's fans with the storied excellence and communal warmth of Ebbets Field.

BROOKLYN DODGERS AT EBBETS FIELD 1913-1957

We now pull our focus away from Ebbets Field with sad regret but happy memories..

The memory of Ebbets Field is not confined solely to architecture or archived playbooks; it is alive, a vibrant, beating pulse, in countless personal stories, in the soft murmur of recollections shared between generations, like precious heirlooms. It exists in faded photographs that hang in coffee shops, their sepia tones hinting at a world now gone, in the twinkle of an old-timer's eye as they recount a game-winning hit, or in the hushed reverence with which modern fans speak of the Brooklyn Dodgers' most significant moments as if speaking of saints. For every fan who ever wept or cheered beneath its lights, for every young hopeful who first discovered the magic of baseball in its stands, their young hearts ignited by the roar of the crowd, Ebbets Field stands immortal, a testimony to the passion and community that birthed the most beautiful game, a love story etched in dust and dreams.

Even as the physical structure gave way to progress and urban transformation, its spirit, imbued in the collective memory of Brooklyn and the very design of modern stadiums, remains a lodestar, a guiding light in the dark. The stories of daring plays, last-minute heroics, and the profound sense of belonging continue to inspire those who look back with nostalgia and step into contemporary ballparks seeking a taste of that unsullied joy and communal celebration. The final out at Ebbets Field is not just a moment in history; it is a symbol, an exclamation point to a saga that refuses to be forgotten, a tearful farewell that became an eternal promise.

In the silence that followed that historic game, as the echoes of the crowd slowly faded into memory, replaced by the chilling quiet of absence, Brooklyn learned that the end of one chapter could give rise to the eternal legacy of a place and a team. The Dodgers, forever intertwined with the soul of Brooklyn, left behind monuments not only of statistics and records but of hope, resilience, and a spirit that continues to ignite hearts long after the final game. As modern ballparks rise and evolve, they stand on the shoulders of that beloved past, drawing inspiration from the grit and grace of Ebbets Field, a silent homage to the ghosts of grandeur.

Now, as fans step through the arched portals of Citi Field or settle into the convivial atmospheres of Camden Yards and Coors Field, they carry with them an awareness that baseball is more than a game—it is a living narrative, a chronicle of moments that define a community, a continuous story of joy and heartbreak. The legacy of Ebbets Field glows like a beacon in that narrative, a constant reminder that true history is written not merely in triumphs on the scoreboard but in the hearts and memories of those who believe in the game's magic, in the unbreakable bond between a team and its people.

Thus, the chapter of Ebbets Field and the Brooklyn Dodgers may have closed on that cool September day, with the final run scored and the last pitch thrown, but its spirit endures a poignant, everlasting song. It lingers in every retelling, every architectural homage, and every time a bat connects with a ball in that ineffable, transcendent dance known as baseball. In every cheering crowd and every whispered memory, the legend of Ebbets Field lives on—a timeless symphony of passion, perseverance, and an undying love for the game, a love that, even through tears, still burns brightly.

Trolleys and Dodgers have left town forever-Brownie instamatic picture taken by Author.

About the Author

Allen Schery has been a devoted Dodger fan since 1952, living through the legendary "Boys of Summer" era and personally knowing many of its stars. Growing up in Brooklyn's loyal working-class community, he witnessed a perfect harmony between the grit of the Dodgers and the resilience of their fans. When the team left Brooklyn in 1957, nine-year-old Allen was left in shock and disbelief—a loss that never fully healed, yet one that made his memories of that era even more treasured.

Those memories inspired a lifetime of research and writing on Dodger history. His works include *The Boys of Spring – The Birth of the Dodgers* (1883–1930), already published. There is a forthcoming book entitled *Ebbets to Paradise: O'Malley's Journey to the Coliseum & Dodger Stadium* (1958–1963) due next month. Upcoming titles include *A Darker Shade of Dodger Blue: The Frank McCourt Story* (2004–2012) already written. He has also outlined *The Real Walter O'Malley Story*, a work intended to correct long-standing inaccuracies in existing accounts.

Libby Pataki governor of New York's wife presents Allen with Award for one of the ten best museums in New York

In addition to his books, Allen shares his passion for baseball history through public speaking and digital media. Some of his SABR presentations can be found on his YouTube channel, where he brings the rich legacy of the Dodgers to life for fans, historians, and researchers alike.

Like the Dodgers, Allen eventually made his way to Los Angeles. He is an active member of SABR (Society of American Baseball Research), specifically the **Allen Roth Division**, and continues to preserve and share the team's history with a unique blend of personal connection, scholarly rigor, and storytelling skill.

Bibliography

Chapter One

Brooklyn Eagle. Jan 3, 1912, pp. 21-22. Brooklyn Eagle. Apr 13, 1913, pp. 23-26. Brooklyn Eagle. Apr 4, 1913, p. 19. Brooklyn Eagle. Apr 6, 1913, pp. 1, 58. Brooklyn Eagle. Apr 9, 1913, pp. 22-26. Saccoman, John. "Charles Ebbets." SABR Paper. New York Tribune. Jan 3, 1912, p. 8. New York Tribune. Jan 3, 1912, p. 8. Brooklyn Eagle. Feb 1, 1912, p. 22. Brooklyn Eagle. Jan 10, 1912, p. 23. Brooklyn Eagle. Feb 10, 1912, p. 1. Brooklyn Eagle. Feb 19, 1912, p. 7. Brooklyn Eagle. Feb 4, 1912, p. 43. New York Times. Apr 6, 1913, p. 13. Brooklyn Daily Times. Apr 13, 1913, p. 13. Brooklyn Eagle. Apr 5, 1913, p. 1. New York Times. Apr 6, 1913, pp. 58-59. Brooklyn Eagle. Apr 11, 1913, p. 2. Brooklyn Eagle. Apr 12, 1913, p. 18. Zinn, John G. Charles Ebbets. McFarland, 2019. Schery, Allen. The Boys of Spring-The Birth of the Dodgers. Grand Central Station Press 2022.

Chapter Two

Brooklyn Eagle. Jan 3, 1912, pp. 21-22. Brooklyn Eagle. Apr 13, 1913, pp. 23-26. Brooklyn Eagle. Apr 4, 1913, p. 19. Brooklyn Eagle. Apr 6, 1913, pp. 1, 58. Brooklyn Eagle. Apr 9, 1913, pp. 22-26. Saccoman, John. "Charles Ebbets." SABR Paper. New York Tribune. Jan 3, 1912, p. 8.

New York Tribune. Jan 3, 1912, p. 8. Brooklyn Eagle. Feb 1, 1912, p. 22. Brooklyn Eagle. Jan 10, 1912, p. 23. Brooklyn Eagle. Feb 10, 1912, p. 1. Brooklyn Eagle. Feb 19, 1912, p. 7. Brooklyn Eagle. Feb 4, 1912, p. 43. New York Times. Apr 6, 1913, p. 13. Brooklyn Daily Times. Apr 13, 1913, p. 13. Brooklyn Eagle. Apr 5, 1913, p. 1. New York Times. Apr 6, 1913, pp. 58-59. Brooklyn Eagle. Apr 11, 1913, p. 2. Brooklyn Eagle. Apr 12, 1913, p. 18. Zinn, John G. Charles Ebbets. McFarland, 2019. Schery, Allen. The Boys Of Spring-The Birth of the Dodgers. Grand Central Station Press 2022.

Chapter Three

Sporting News. Apr 13, 1916, p. 5. Brooklyn Eagle. Oct 5, 1916, p. 25. New York Sun. Sep 22, 1916, p. 22. Washington Post. Oct 9, 1916, p. 8. Brooklyn Eagle. Oct 11, 1916, p. 25. Sporting Life. Nov 18, 1916, p. 6. Brooklyn Eagle. Oct 17, p. 6. Evening World. Oct 4, 1916, p. 12. New York Tribune. Oct 21, 1916, p. 15. New York Sun. Jun 24, 1919, p. 2. Brooklyn Eagle. Jul 6, 1917, p. 1. Brooklyn Eagle. Sep 24, 1917, p. 1. Brooklyn Eagle. Jan 9, 1918, p. 20. New York Sun. Aug 18, 1919, p. 17. New York Sun. Aug 18, 1919, p. 17. Brooklyn Eagle. May 5, 1919, p. 18. Schery, Allen. The Boys Of Spring-The Birth of the Dodgers. Grand Central Station Press 2022.Brooklyn Eagle. May 12, 1920, p. 67. Brooklyn Eagle. May 3, 1920, p. 18. Brooklyn Eagle. Sep 29, 1920, p. 18. Brooklyn Eagle. Oct 4, 1920, p. 1. Brooklyn Eagle. Sep 21, 1920, p. 20. Brooklyn Eagle. Oct 3, 1920, p. 64. Brooklyn Eagle. Oct 6, 1920, p. 22. Brooklyn Eagle. Oct 8, 1920, p. 24. Mansch, Larry. Rube Marquard-The Life and Times of a Baseball Hall of Famer. McFarland, 1998. Brooklyn Eagle. Oct 11, 1920, p. 1. New York Herald. Sep 27, p. 8. Brooklyn Eagle. Oct 10, 1920, p. 1. Brooklyn Eagle.

Oct 11, 1920, p. 20. Brooklyn Eagle. Oct 13, 1920, p. 22. Brooklyn Eagle. Oct 21, 1920, p. 20.

Chapter Four

New York Daily News. Sep 28, 1941, pp. 194-196. Parrott, Harold. The Lords of Baseball. Praeger, 1976. This great Game website. "The thirties." New York Times. "Stephen McKeever Dies In Brooklyn - President of the Dodgers Club in National League Victim of Pneumonia at 84 - In Baseball Since 1912 - Succeeded Frank B. York as Leader - He and Brother Built Ebbets Field." Mar 7, 1938, p. 17. Schery, Allen. The Boys Of Spring-The Birth of the Dodgers. Grand Central Station Press 2022.

Chapter Five

Skipper, John. Zack Wheat. Iowa History Journal. Appel, Marty. Zack Wheat. Memories & Dreams. Nash, Ogden. "Line-Up for Yesterday" poem. Sport Magazine, January 1949. Healey, Mark. Zack Wheat. Gotham Baseball. Posnanski, Joe. Zack Wheat. The Hardball Times - FanGraphs. James, Bill. Zack Wheat. The Hardball Times - FanGraphs.

Chapter Six

Saccoman, John. "Charlie Ebbets." SABR Paper. Schery, Allen. The Boys of Spring- The Birth of the Dodgers. Grand Central Station Press 2022.. New York Times. "Robinson Elected Robins' President - Unanimously Chosen by Brooklyn Club Stockholders to Succeed the Late C.H . Ebbets - Also to Remain Manager - Makes Wheat His Assistant and Names Fournier Captain - Heydler Lauds Selection." May 26, 1925, p. 17. Drebinger, John. "McKeever Becomes Head Of Dodgers - 78-Old Half

Owner Succeeds York, Who Resigns as President of Club - Other Officers Elected - Gilleaudeau and Mulvey Chosen as Vice Presidents at Reorganization Meeting." New York Times. Oct 13, 1932, p. 27. New York Times. "Stephen McKeever Dies In Brooklyn - President of the Dodgers Club in National League Victim of Pneumonia at 84 - In Baseball Since 1912 - Succeeded Frank B. York as Leader - He and Brother Built Ebbets Field." Mar 7, 1938, p. 17. McGee, Bob. The Greatest Ballpark Ever: Ebbets Field and the Story of the Brooklyn Dodgers. Riverdale, 2005. Schery, Allen. The Boys Of Spring-The Birth of the Dodgers. Grand Central Station Press 2022.

Chapter Seven

Society for American Baseball Research. "Walter O'Malley." Britannica. "Walter O'Malley | Los Angeles Dodgers, MLB Owner." D'Antonio, Michael. Forever Blue: The True Story of Walter O'Malley, Baseball's Most Controversial Owner. Riverhead Books, 2009. Sullivan, Neil J. The Dodgers Move West. Oxford University Press, 1987. Golenbock, Peter. Bums: An Oral History of the Brooklyn Dodgers. Pocket Books, 1984. Shapiro, Michael. The Last Good Season: Brooklyn, the Dodgers, and Their Final Pennant Race Together. Doubleday, 2003. Walter O'Malley. com (both Peter O'Malley and Brent Shyer personally).

Chapter Eight

Society for American Baseball Research. "Larry MacPhail." Encyclopedia.com. "MacPhail, Leland Stanford, Sr." Honig, Donald. The Baseball Hall of Fame 50th Anniversary Book. Collier Books, 1989. Sullivan, Neil J. The

Dodgers Move West. Oxford University Press, 1987. Golenbock, Peter. Bums: An Oral History of the Brooklyn Dodgers. Pocket Books, 1984.

Chapter Nine

Society for American Baseball Research. "Leo Durocher." Don't Give Me No Lip: The Cultural and Religious Roots of Leo Durocher's Competitiveness. Durocher, Leo. Nice Guys Finish Last. Simon and Schuster, 1975. Thomson, Bobby, and Lee Heiman. The Giants Win the Pennant, The Giants Win the Pennant!. Zebra Books, 1991. Sullivan, Neil J. The Dodgers Move West. Oxford University Press, 1987.

Chapter Ten

Rampersad, Arnold. Jackie Robinson: A Biography. Alfred A. Knopf, 1997. Robinson, Sharon. Promises to Keep: How Jackie Robinson Changed America. Scholastic Press, 2004. Kennedy, Kostya. True: The Four Seasons of Jackie Robinson. Random House, 2016. Simon, Scott. Jackie Robinson and the Integration of Baseball. Wiley, 2002.

Chapter Eleven

Society for American Baseball Research (SABR). "Branch Rickey Bio." Library of Congress. "Branch Rickey Papers." Brooklyn Eagle Archives. Walter O'Malley.com (both Peter O'Malley and Brent Shyer personally). Lowenfish, Lee. Branch Rickey: Baseball's Ferocious Gentleman. University of Nebraska Press, 2007. Polner, Murray. Branch Rickey: A Biography. Atheneum, 1982. Monteleone, John J., ed. Branch Rickey's Little Blue Book. Touchstone, 1995. Rickey, Branch, and Robert Riger. The American Diamond: A Documentary of the Game of Baseball. Simon and Schuster, 1965. Sullivan, Neil J. The Dodgers Move West. Oxford University Press, 1987.

Chapter Twelve

NYU Special Collections. "Walter O'Malley Brooklyn Dodgers Records." Brooklyn Eagle Archives. Society for American Baseball Research (SABR). "Brooklyn Dodgers and Walter O'Malley pages." Walter O'Malley.com (both Peter O'Malley and Brent Shyer personally). Sullivan, Neil J. The Dodgers Move West. Oxford University Press, 1987. D'Antonio, Michael. Forever Blue: The True Story of Walter O'Malley, Baseball's Most Controversial Owner. Riverhead Books, 2009. Podair, Jerald. City of Dreams: Dodger Stadium and the Birth of Modern Los Angeles. Princeton University Press, 2017. Kahn, Roger. The Boys of Summer. Harper & Row, 1972.

Chapter Thirteen

Brooklyn Public Library. "Brooklyn Dodgers Research Guide (Brooklyn Dodgers Collection)." Brooklyn Eagle Archives. Baseball-Reference.com. "Brooklyn Dodgers History (Brooklyn Dodgers Team Stats)." Society for American Baseball Research (SABR). "Brooklyn Dodgers pages." Marzano, Rudy. The Last Years of the Brooklyn Dodgers: A History, 1950-1957. McFarland, 2005. Golenbock, Peter. Bums: An Oral History of the Brooklyn Dodgers. Pocket Books, 1984. McGee, Robert M. The Greatest Ballpark Ever: Ebbets Field and the Story of the Brooklyn Dodgers. Riverdale, 2005. Kahn, Roger. The Boys of Summer. Harper & Row, 1972.

Chapter Fourteen

Brooklyn Eagle Archives. Society for American Baseball Research (SABR). "Brooklyn Dodgers pages." Walter O'Malley.com (both Peter O'Malley and Brent Shyer personally). Sullivan, Neil J. The Dodgers Move West. Oxford University Press, 1987. D'Antonio, Michael. Forever Blue: The True Story of Walter O'Malley, Baseball's Most Controversial Owner. Riverhead Books, 2009. Podair, Jerald. City of Dreams: Dodger Stadium and the Birth of Modern Los Angeles. Princeton University Press, 2017. Caro, Robert A. The Power Broker: Robert Moses and the Fall of New York. Alfred A. Knopf, 1974.

Chapter Fifteen

New York Public Library. "Brooklyn Dodgers Collection." Society for American Baseball Research (SABR). "Brooklyn Dodgers/Ebbets Field resources." Brooklyn Eagle Archives. Marzano, Rudy. The Last Years of the Brooklyn Dodgers: A History, 1950-1957. McFarland, 2005. Kahn, Roger. The Boys of Summer. Harper & Row, 1972. Golenbock, Peter. Bums: An Oral History of the Brooklyn Dodgers. Pocket Books, 1984.

Chapter Sixteen

New York Public Library. "Brooklyn Dodgers Collection." Brooklyn Eagle Archives. Society for American Baseball Research (SABR). "Ebbets Field Resources." This Day in Baseball. "The Destruction of Ebbets Field." Zinn, John G., Paul G. Zinn, and David Cicotello, eds. Ebbets Field: Essays and Memories of Brooklyn's Historic Ballpark, 1913-1960. McFarland, 2013. Marzano, Rudy. The Last Years of the Brooklyn Dodgers: A History, 1950-1957. McFarland, 2005. Golenbock, Peter. Bums: An Oral History of the Brooklyn Dodgers. Pocket Books, 1984.

Chapters Seventeen and Eighteen

Come out of Author's Personal Memory

Production Notes and Compliance Statement

This book and all accompanying materials have been created with full respect for copyright and intellectual property laws.

• All written content is original or properly licensed.

• Historical photographs and memorabilia come from my personally owned collection spanning over 75 years, predating the licensing of agencies such as Getty Images and Alamy.

• Licensed Associated Press (AP) photographs from 1991 and images from trusted sources like WalterOmalley.com have been included with proper permission.

• All software tools used—Atticus, Microsoft, Microsoft Word, Grammarly AI, Affinity Photo 2, Paint Shop Pro 2023, and Textract—were legally purchased and used according to their licenses.

• Research was conducted via reputable sources like Google Search to ensure accuracy. Also included was Newspapers.com

I have complied fully with Kindle Direct Publishing's guidelines and all applicable laws.

Any attempt to dispute the legality of this work without valid evidence will be met with strong legal defense, including action against frivolous claims and abuse of process.

Made in the USA
Columbia, SC
10 October 2025

3dd47c6c-2ad4-49e7-8c55-225c4c11911fR01